Your ~~Life is~~
In Your Hands

Your Life Is
In Your Hands

*Practical Palm Reading
for Purposeful Living*

Kay Packard

2015 · Pioneer Press
Three Rivers, California

ISBN 978-0-9907179-0-4

Pioneer Press
Post Office Box 321
Three Rivers, California 93271

for
Rosemary

Acknowledgements

THIS WORK is founded on many hundreds, if not thousands, of years of palmistry, a century of scientific hand reading, and more recently, four decades of hand analysis practiced and taught by my teacher, Richard Unger. I gratefully acknowledge countless practitioners and pioneers, especially Richard, along with his wife, Alana Unger, and my mentor Vernon Mahabal, for the love and dedication each have put into this sacred art and science.

The actual writing of this book has spanned beyond three years, and numerous people have contributed. Thank you to the owners of the handprints in this book for inviting me to hear and print your incredible stories substantiating the interpretations of the markings in the hands. Many thanks also to the owners of the thousands of hands I have read along with hearing your personal stories over the last decade, beginning with my mother, Rosemary. My abiding appreciation to my students for your questions that have helped me clarify curricula and for generously opening your hearts so fully and expressing some of your best and most difficult life experiences linked with the etchings in your palms and fingerprints. To you, life-long friends Teddi Sue Johnson, Tracy Owen Chapman and Lora Gomes, and to my brothers, Ben and Cliff Packard, sister, Jane Hardiman, and uncle Dr. Andrew Comrey for offering your unswerving encouragement. Tracy, thank you also for your professional insight on public perception, preparation, and reception.

Many thanks to my friends, colleagues, and students who reviewed pieces of, or the entire manuscript: Pam Lockhart, Trude Xanders, Peggy Arvidson, Ellyn Daly, Clarinda Sayre, and especially Debé Wenig, Jane Hardiman, Linda Salazar, and Anne Bunnell, who offered extensive edits for clarity and understanding. There are too many to name who I thank for your candid feedback during title testing. To colleagues Jena Griffiths, Markus Thorndike, Mary DeLave, Janet Savage, Pamelah Landers, Baeth Davis, and Ronelle Coburn I thank you for your mutual support, inspiration, and persistence in advancing hand analysis into the world. A special thank you to editors Eric Larson and Angela Renkowski for all of your effort. Eric, your questions and meticulous attention to details boosted my confidence to new levels for an exceptional project result. I am honored to show original art by Wendy McKeller on the cover design; thank you, Wendy. I am blessed with many friends who have cheered me on during this process; to all of you, thank you! And to Raymond Velasquez, for your love and spiritual insight; I thank you for your unceasing enthusiasm, encouragement for me to keep at it, and for your vision of the arising outreach of the contents herein. Thank you all for believing in me and helping me to live my most meaningful and incredibly rich life.

Contents

Preface

AT THE ENDS of your arms, etched into the palms of your hands, is a map for you to successfully make your life into a masterpiece. Yes, your hands are inscribed with secret symbols that, once deciphered, can reveal the path to your most meaningful life. With a little information and some practice, you can easily learn to decode these messages about yourself and use them to live the optimum life you were meant to live.

As a former faculty member at the International Institute of Hand Analysis, and as the founder and director of the American Academy of Hand Analysis, I have taught the principles of reading hands to many students as well as clients in my own hand analysis practice. These students have delved deeply into their own lives, not only to see who they truly are, but also to awaken to and to clearly articulate their life-missions and purposes—what they are here to do. I have seen people transform their lives with a deeper understanding of themselves gained through learning the secret language embedded in their own hands. I have witnessed students and clients expand their awareness, express themselves from their essential Selves, and awaken to and claim their personal power. I have been blessed to observe each person's "a-ha" moment. After being given a short reading, one client exclaimed, "I am amazed by the accuracy!" One beginning student immediately recognized, "We're teaching our minds to work more positively." Another new student said, "What I'm reading in my hands *totally fits!*"

To extend these rewards to the world is my purpose in writing this book—to help guide you into your own transformation and to a life lived on purpose. This book is based on more than 200 hours of content-rich course material I have developed, practiced, and taught to students around the world since 2003. It is easy to understand, logical, and it offers quick insights. You will see how to interpret specific sign-posts in your hands and read the life-map written on your hands and on those of your friends, family, and clients. What I teach you will assist you in weaving together both the understood and misunderstood aspects of yourself so that you can manifest a balanced life—now.

My objective is to open you to the possibility of relating to your natural Self more deeply, confidently, and powerfully. You have extraordinary potential that is calling out to come through you. I'm not asking you to take my word for it; I'm asking you to try it for yourself, and see how it works for you; see how your life is positively transformed.

Have fun experimenting with the knowledge you receive from your own two hands. Reach inward and unlock your wisdom. Your life-map potential literally decorates your hands. See it, cultivate it—and illuminate! It's your time to shine. Your destiny is all in your hands—clearly.

Your Life Is
In Your Hands

Introduction

"Whatever be the means adopted, you
must at least return to the Self, so why not
abide as the Self here and now?"
—Ramana Maharshi

IF YOU HAVE EVER thought that you might like to see more deeply into who you truly are, this book is for you. *Your Life Is In Your Hands* is about you mining the treasures buried in your hands and chiseling, shaping, and sculpting your best life. This begins with you using the wisdom revealed by the inscriptions in your hands, then taking control of your life and getting from where you are to where you want to be. I hope the new way of looking at your life that I offer in this book inspires you to:

+ Tune into your true nature—the Self
+ Look at yourself and accept who you're seeing
+ Understand your personal motives and make conscious life choices
+ Clearly recognize and fully embrace your strengths and weaknesses
+ Learn a foolproof method for capitalizing on your weaknesses to boost your talents
+ Free yourself from outdated and negative thought-patterns
+ Advance your life-purpose through self-examination and integration
+ Reclaim your power for living *your* best life
+ Aim high and take charge!

As you better understand yourself through pondering the various markings in your hands and making sense of them, you can take consistent charge of your life. Are you ready to take an honest look at yourself? Have you wondered who you are and what you are here to do? Have you taken an honest inventory of your talents, skills, and gifts? Are you applying those attributes as best you can for your most fulfilling life? The whole point of this book is to help you answer these questions in a way that assists you in living a life of meaning, starting right here and now. All that is required is a little curiosity, a thirst for freedom, and an open mind.

I would like to make one thing clear before going any further: I'm not offering a method of fortune-telling, psychic reading, or predictive techniques. This is about you discovering and listening to your truth. Your hands have very specific etchings that are the result of the neurological byways and highways that race through your brain waves and psyche. The topography of the skin on your palms and fingers can be decoded to reveal your special talents, attributes, preferences, and strengths, as well as your weaknesses and challenges. Attractions, distractions, and irritations in your emotional, physical, mental, and spiritual realms can be identified and interpreted. Ideal career and relationship scenarios can be revealed.

Be aware also that the lines in your hands are not permanent, but can change. That's right—they can change. Markings appear and disappear with time. The system you'll be learning focuses on what is present at the time you look at the hands. Each marking has a positive and a negative interpretation. The positive interpretation describes your innate capacity operating at its fullest potential. The negative interpretation relates to a quality that is either under- or overused.

All negative possibilities offer shadow wisdom. Shadows are created by light. We grow stronger as we open to our weaknesses and shine the light of awareness on them. You'll learn to use your weaknesses, bring them to the light, and bloom into your most amazing life.

You'll find a "mantra" associated with most of the markings described in this book. I use the word "mantra" to imply the integration of the positive and negative interpretations of these markings into affirmational statements. Derived directly from the markings, the mantras are intended to uplift you into realizing your highest potential.

Within this book, expect to find precise and reliable information for interpreting the God-given symbols in your hands. I encourage you to keep a notebook to accompany your reading so that you have plenty of space to record your newfound awareness as you unearth your treasures. In essence, you are in charge of defining your destiny. This book will show you how.

1. The Basics of Hand Analysis

Learning the Lay of the Land

> *"On the hand of every earthling man*
> *he puts a seal*
> *For every mortal man to know his*
> *work."*
>
> —*Job 37:7*

WITHIN YOUR magnificent hands are many features to explore. The shape, fingers, lines, and markings in the hand can be interpreted to define particular elements of your personality and psychology. Blending a combination of two or more markings together will illustrate how you are different from everyone else. I'd like to introduce you to some fundamentals of hand analysis here. It's simple to get started. Depending on your desire and motivation, advanced levels can also be mastered. But in this book, we'll keep it simple.

The basic hand map (Figure 1) shows the primary landscape of the hand. The high-level descriptions of the fingers and mounts come from the ancient art and science of hand reading. You will be introduced to an expanded yet simple vocabulary as you read through this book. The major lines are also identified in Figure 1. You may want to bookmark this map so that you can quickly refer back to it as you read more about the basic features of hands.

Areas of the hand such as the fingers, mounts, and lines mold themselves according to how you engage particular traits in your own life. You are a whole being with a whole hand—times two! Just as the hand is compartmentalized, you too can be recognized by just a few of the attributes in your interior makeup that reflect externally out into

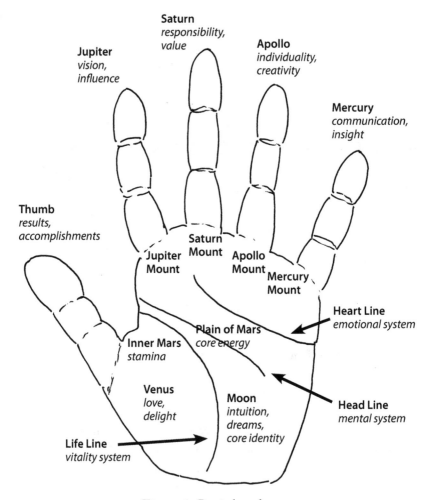

Figure 1: Basic hand map

the world. But when all of your attributes are blended together, you get a more complete picture of yourself, inside and out.

For example:

If the shape, height, and quality of your index finger is strong and dominant, you have an aptitude to influence others based on your higher vision.

If your Moon Mount is full and well marked, you place importance on deeper meaning and intuition.

If the Heart Line on one of your hands curves up toward your index finger, you are big-hearted and caring.

Those are only single and limited attributes, however. Blending these three attributes together reveals an aptitude for intuitive leadership with care. The Dalai Lama comes to mind as I weave together leadership, intuition, and care.

Let's look at another example using the thumb. The thumb shows one's will to succeed and ability to get results. Imagine life without a thumb. What wouldn't get done? Every single person uses his or her thumb energy in a completely different way. If someone has a large thumb relative to the rest of the hand, and if it is naturally splayed away from the hand, that person will generally prefer to grasp and handle elements of life on a large scale. Conversely, a person with a smaller thumb held more tightly to the palm will be more inclined to solitude and will be content with less to do.

It is important not to assess someone based on only one characteristic. Rather, look at a variety of markings to determine a more accurate picture. Think of an individual ant contributing to the whole colony. We can't get a whole picture of the ant colony by looking at only one of the six-legged workers. To appreciate the power of the colony, it would be better to study the interactions between the moving insects and analyze their operations to understand their purpose. Individual ants creating a colony are like the single features of the hands coming together to illustrate the whole.

You might ask, "How do I read the right versus the left hand?" As a general rule, the right hand is considered your active hand and will be read to show how you present yourself to the outer world. For example, motives and personality traits that you express at work and in public will be read primarily from your right hand. Conversely, the left hand is considered the passive, reflective, and introspective hand and reveals your personality at home, in private, where you wear your fuzzy slippers and comfy robe. For example, preferences in intimate relationships will be read primarily from your left hand.

The exception to these general rules is when a person uses his or her left hand the majority of the time (writing, throwing a ball, swinging a bat, or using a shovel in the garden) *and* when the left hand is more eye-catching than the right hand, like a ripe piece of fruit versus an unripe one. Seeing this level of detail often requires a handprint. For now, consider your right hand your active, public hand and your left hand your private, reflective hand.

Fingers are like antennae, receiving and transmitting energy. As shown in Figure 1, each finger correlates to a mythological archetype, which will be explained in Chapter 6. The straighter the finger, the more likely it is that the energy related to that finger will flow into and out of your life. It is more common, however, for the fingers to be slightly tilted or curved. If one of your fingers is bent or damaged in some way, the energy related to that finger will be impeded, like a rushing river with a bend that slows and deviates the flow of water.

The mounts on the palm represent reservoirs of energy. The higher a mount rises on your palm, the more prominent that energy will be in your life. Hold your hand at eye level, palm up, and notice which mount is tallest and fullest. The description of the finger above that mount indicates the kind of energy to which you have access.

The skin carvings, called dermatoglyphics, in our fingerprints also reflect an energy imprint. These patterns, or codes, can be analyzed, deciphered, and translated from "palmese" into words that describe your soul's curriculum—what you're here to learn so that you can evolve as a soul having a human experience. The markings in the palm indicate how one can directly support the soul's curriculum.

Charlatans and misguided palmists have given palm reading a bad name. Predictive readings and forecasts of future predicaments and certain doom were said to be inevitable. You've probably heard of an untrained and unethical palmist who predicts the length of a person's life based on the length of his or her Life Line. Let me make it very clear: this is an absurdity, and untrue.

This sort of quackery is not unique to palmistry. A small number of doctors, lawyers, auto mechanics, and gurus have made their professions look bad. Probably most do so without intending to; but the damage is done, all the same.

As we give attention to things in our lives, we consciously and oftentimes unconsciously, imagine award-winning life-movie scenes. My life movie as a Pioneer involves, but is not limited to, innovative teaching with great passion as an inspirational messenger. You, too, follow a theme in your life-movie. Your reason for being is embedded in your hands. Take a look. What do you see?

To get the best outcomes from your life-movie, it's important to be curious, ask questions, follow your intuition, take personal responsibility for your investigations, and perform according to a well-written script. Ultimately, you and your God (or whatever you place your faith in) are the author of your script. To have a more informed opinion of palmistry and hand analysis you are wise to read about the subject and visit with highly qualified, certified, and professional hand analysts.

At this basic level of hand analysis, I focus on a non-predictive and accurate approach to decoding the natural line formations, hand and finger shapes, and unique fingerprint patterns. As mentioned above, there are positive and negative interpretations to each identifiable attribute of the hands. Each characteristic of the hand, be it the Heart Line, dominant finger, hand shape, or Life Line, has both positive and negative connotations. Consider, for example, someone with an affinity for wine tasting. The positive possibility is that the person will become an expert wine taster, with regularly featured reviews in wine-tasting magazines. The negative possibility is that the person will drink too much, and lose the ability to apply his expertise. Assimilating both sides is crucial for complete understanding, awareness, and development.

How to Take Hand Prints

Before starting, please read through the instructions and see the hand and fingerprint samples at the end. You may want to watch the short video "How to Take a Hand Print" at http://YourLifeIsInYourHands Book.com/services/print-your-hands. If you have any cuts or open wounds on either of your hands, please wait until they are healed before printing your hands.

Disposable pre-inked sheets are available from the AAHA office (clients e-mail packard.kay@gmail.com).

Materials
    One set of two 6" x 10" ink sheets
    4 to 6 pieces of 8½" x 11" paper
    Paper towels
    Soap and gentle scouring pad to wash ink off hands after printing

Instructions
    1. Remove jewelry. Wash hands and let dry.

2. Lay out materials on countertop near a sink with running warm water.

3. Carefully pull apart the pre-inked sheets by pulling the top sheet away from the bottom sheet at one of the corners.

4. Turn over the top sheet of pre-inked paper so that both inked sides are facing up, next to each other on the counter.

5. Lay your right hand on one of the pre-inked sheets. Firmly press on the back of your hand so that your palm and fingers are pressed into the ink. With the sheet of inked paper stuck to your hand, lift your hand and *press the inked paper into the center of your palm and fingers*. Move the inked sheet around your hand so that the ink is distributed evenly over your hand. Your entire palm, fingers, and fingertips should all be well coated with ink. Pull the inked paper off of your hand and be sure your entire hand is covered in ink. Reapply the same ink sheet if needed to any area of your hand that is missing ink. Set the inked paper aside.

6. With your inked hand and fingers in a comfortable and natural position, press your hand onto a sheet of plain paper. Lay your hand onto the paper beginning with the base of the palm, firmly pressing down as you progress to the top of the palm and the fingers, ending with the upper sections of the fingers. Lift your hand, with the paper attached, and gently press up underneath the paper so that it presses into the center of your palm.

7. Pull the paper off your hand and set your handprint aside. Make sure you have a print of the entire hand, including the center of the palm and the fingers, as much as possible. If not, you can use the same pre-inked sheet to reapply more ink and take a second print. Sometimes the center of the palm does not print, but that's okay; do the best you can do.

8. Print *each fingertip* on the bottom of the sheet with your handprint (Figures 2 and 3). Start with the thumb. Place the thumb on the inked sheet of paper so as to cover the entire upper section of the thumb. Then press the inked thumb onto the handprint sheet, at the bottom of the page under the thumb. Repeat for each finger in order. Label each of your fingerprints as noted in Figure 3.

9. Wash your hand with soap, warm water, and a scrubbing pad (if needed).

10. With your left hand, repeat steps 5 through 9, using the other half of the same pair of pre-inked sheets and another piece of plain paper.

11. Write your name and the date on all handprint sheets. Let your handprints dry before stacking them together.

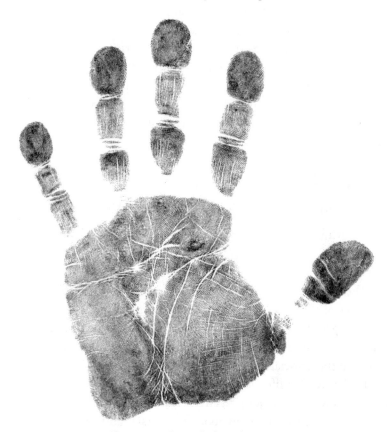

Figure 2: Sample handprint

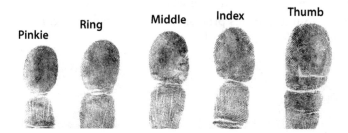

Figure 3: Sample fingerprints

The Major Lines of the Palm

The Heart, Head and Life lines are the major lines of the palm. (See Figure 1 on page 22.) These lines represent the rivers of consciousness relating to particular areas of your life, and reflect how and where you connect with the world. For example, the Heart Line represents your love style and emotional preferences; it is associated with the element Water, which rules the feelings, as emotions ebb and flow like water. The Head Line reflects your thinking system; it is associated with the element Air, which rules the mental process, as information flows through the air. The Life Line corresponds to your body's vitality system; it is associated with the element Earth, which is associated with productivity.

Major Line	System	Element
Heart	Emotional	Water
Head	Thinking	Air
Life	Vitality	Earth

These lines indicate the perceptions, inclinations, preferences, and character of their owner in their respective systems. The more deeply a line is carved into the hand, the more powerful the disposition and tendencies related to that system is. Shallow lines illustrate less inclination to the associated system.

In day-to-day life we constantly engage all three of the systems associated with the major palm lines. Take for instance a simple trip to the local grocery store to buy food for yourself and your family. Emotionally, you imagine what your family will experience while sharing the food you buy. Mentally, you may think about the nutritional value of the foods you select, or even where the food came from. While this is often an unconscious process, you may recall the primary purpose of food, which is to sustain life.

2. The Heart Line

Relationship Symbols, Stories, and Strategies

> *"When you accept yourself the whole world accepts you."*
>
> —Lao Tzu

RELATIONSHIPS CONSUME the majority of our waking lives. Every day we have hundreds of opportunities to connect with other people, including our mates, children, parents, grandparents, siblings, coworkers, bosses, subordinates, business partners, and more. Our best relationships start with ourselves.

You can deepen your understanding of your own or someone else's essential relationship or love style by reading one line in the hand— the Heart Line. The simple knowledge you glean from this etching can pick up, perk up, and improve your daily interactions. Imagine understanding and embracing your emotional system more intimately and improving your relationships by even ten percent.

Your emotional system began its development in the womb. We now know that embryos are affected by relaxing music, car horns, laughing or shouting family members, and any number of other stimuli. After birth, there are an infinite number of environmental factors that continue to influence emotional growth. Our emotions meander and change from day to day, so think of the Heart Line as a river flowing across a plain. As we mature and change, the shape, length, and quality of the Heart Line can and most likely will change as well. You can read your river of the Heart Line to accurately describe your emotional character, tendencies, and requirements.

Non-negotiable needs in relationships—such as the need for

freedom, connection, consideration, or stimulation—are depicted in the Heart Line. It's important you know these needs and that you can claim them for yourself as part of loving yourself. If you can clarify and ask for what you need in a relationship, you're more likely to have that need met. And when you love yourself and your needs are met, you can connect with others more deeply and completely, and therefore appreciate others in a more loving and compassionate way.

This chapter introduces you to four basic, easy-to-read Heart Line types: the Passionate, Big Heart, Hermit, and Rational Romantic. Each represents a style of emotional behavior that is typically displayed to others. How you like to be treated in relationship and how you like to treat others can be read in this line.

Be curious and open to understanding this information, and practice becoming aware of your needs and articulating them in relationships. Be sensitive to others' needs as well. The motivations for connection are different in different people.

I have seen many people who courageously claim their true heart language and live it. It does take bravery to be who you are meant to be. It's not easy, but I'm here to say that living authentically leads to your best life with the most authentic relationships.

Heart Line Identification: Discovering the Heart Line

The Heart Line starts on the outer edge of the palm, under the pinkie finger, and runs horizontally across the hand. (See Figure 4.) The line may be long or short, straight or curved. It usually ends somewhere beneath the middle or index finger. Any Heart Line style is possible on a hand. You may also find a different Heart Line on each hand. The type of Heart Line is independent of culture, gender, or sexual preference. That means any type of Heart Line can show up on any person from any country, man or woman, gay or straight, etc.

The shape of the Heart Line indicates preferred characteristics when relating to others. Curvy lines belong to expressive people who typically show their feelings easily. The Big Heart and Passionate types have curvy lines. They exhibit their feelings more than those with flat or straight Heart Lines. Straight lines belong to people who are more reserved. They reveal their feelings reluctantly. The Hermit and

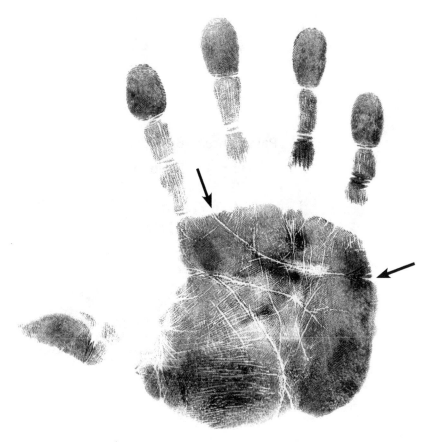

Figure 4: Long, curving Heart Line

Rational Romantic types have flat Heart Lines. They are less likely to display their emotions outwardly.

The description of your style in relationships is determined by the termination point(s) of your Heart Line. Since 2003, I've used the method of placing an imaginary cross on the palm, as taught by my teacher, Richard Unger, to precisely establish where the Heart Line ends. (See Figure 5.) Find where the widest part of the line ends. Sometimes the line will thin out near the end. To be most precise with your reading, locate the quadrant where the *thickest* part of the Heart Line ends. You'll sometimes see a Heart Line fork into two lines, or even split into three lines; we'll learn more on these splits later in this chapter.

You will want to employ this method on both your right and left

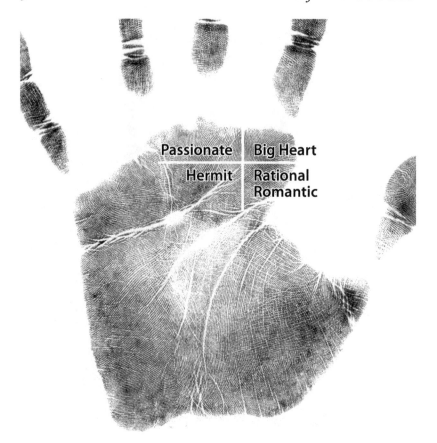

Passionate | Big Heart
Hermit | Rational
Romantic

Figure 5: Names associated with
termination points of the Heart Line

hands. Empirical evidence shows that the Heart Line on the right hand demonstrates the emotional characteristics displayed to the world, whereas the left hand most often shows the traits used at home and in the inner, more intimate world.

The imaginary cross creates four quadrants. To position the cross, draw an imaginary line straight down between the index and middle finger. Decide whether the Heart Line ends on the index or the middle finger side of the vertical line. Next draw an imaginary horizontal line across the vertical line about half an inch from base of the fingers. Now determine whether the Heart Line ends above or below the horizontal line.

Using this method, look to see where the Heart Line terminates on each hand. The Heart Line type is named according to where the line ends. These line-types correspond to the elements of nature—Earth, Water, Air, and Fire. The names illustrate emotional behaviors found in owners of these lines. As an example, the Heart Line in Figure 5 is short, flat, and ends in the lower quadrant formed by the imaginary cross below the middle finger. This is called the Hermit Heart.

The Passionate Heart

The Passionate Heart Line, associated with the element Fire, curves up toward the middle finger (Figure 6). It touches the top of the palm and ends in the upper quadrant formed by the imaginary cross under the middle finger.

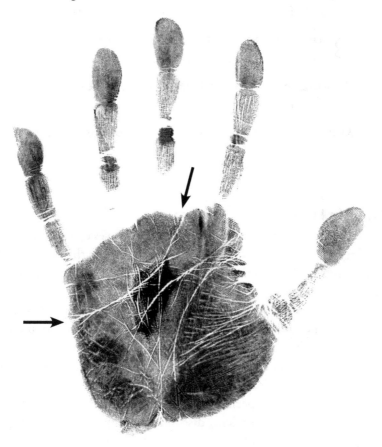

Figure 6: The Passionate Heart

If you are the Passionate Heart, you are likely enthusiastic, expressive, excitable, and even flirtatious. You have the charisma to be the life of the party. Your natural design is like a campfire, attracting people to your warmth. It's crucial for you to express your wants, even when others don't appreciate your directness. You tend to be happiest when you do expose your desires. Your biggest challenge is being stuck with people you consider boring. You can be so intense that when you feel something passionately, it shows loudly and clearly. A word of caution: that little campfire can turn into a forest fire if not contained or given appropriate outlet. I remind the Passionate Heart to display his or her wildest passions *and* be considerate of the needs of others.

> **Key Words:** Enthusiasm, expressiveness, spontaneity, changeability, inspiration, impulsiveness, volatility
>
> **Passionate Heart Positive:** I bring excitement and charisma to the scene.
>
> **Passionate Heart Negative:** I can forget the emotional needs of others.
>
> **Mantra:** I am claiming my desires and expressing my passion with grace and consideration.

The Big Heart

The Big Heart, coupled to the element Water, curves up toward the index finger. It touches the top of the palm and ends in the upper quadrant formed by the imaginary cross under the index finger, or closer to the index finger than the middle finger.

If you are a Big Heart, you feel emotions keenly and are warmhearted, caring, and nurturing of others. You are a Sweetheart and like connecting with other people and animals. Your favorite song might be "All You Need Is Love" by the Beatles. Your natural design is like a water droplet that joins the pool at the base of a waterfall. Seeing others bond during a special gathering warms your heart. Your feelings are hurt if people suddenly disconnect with you or if you witness detachment and conflict between loved ones. Your biggest challenge is to nurture yourself along with others and not fall victim to emotional

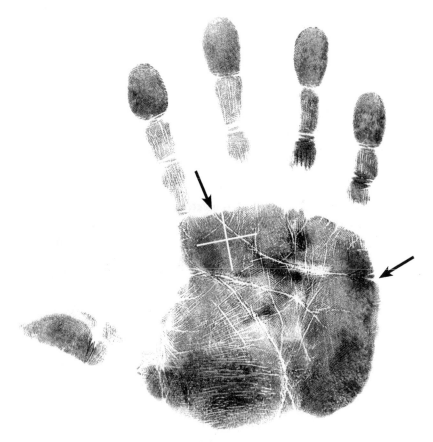

Figure 7: The Big Heart

sell-out. If, in your view, someone disconnects from you abruptly, you might take it personally and become overly critical of yourself, blaming yourself (or the other) for the separation. I remind the Big Heart to look at the truth of the separation or change in the relationship to help him accept himself and all his feelings in all stages of the relationship.

Key Words: Caring, compassion, connectedness, charitableness, self-sacrifice, martyrdom

Big Heart Positive: I help people feel loved and cared for, while spending some time alone nurturing myself.

Big Heart Negative: I can easily lose myself in the drama of others and feel like a victim.

Mantra: I claim my boundaries, realizing I am the love
I seek and long to embody.

The Hermit Heart

The short and straight Heart Line belongs to the Hermit and is associated with the element Earth. It ends in the lower quadrant formed
by the imaginary cross below the middle finger. (The upper arrow in
Figure 8 points to another line that looks like it could be a Heart Line,
but it is not; these lines are not connected.)

If you are a Hermit, you are a lone settler. This doesn't mean you
will always be alone or that you want to go through life solo. It does
mean that you require sanctuary time. The Hermit certainly has emotions, but you display yours less than do owners of curved Heart Lines.

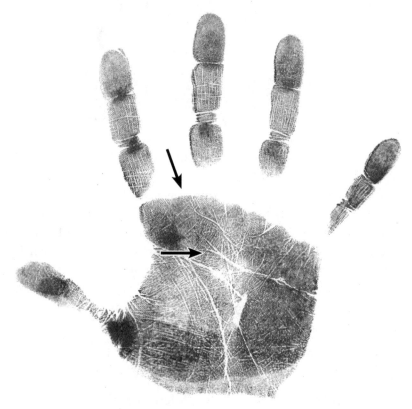

Figure 8: The Hermit Heart

You need time to marinate in your feelings before responding to emotional stimulation. You like loyal, solid, and dependable relationships in which you have a strong sense of freedom. In fact, freedom is non-negotiable to you. Your nature is to be productive and grounded. Privacy, security, and work are high priorities. You show your love by doing things for others. You assure protection for those few you are loyal to. You might not ask others "How are you feeling?" because you believe that actions speak louder than words. You simply look at how people are doing, without becoming entangled in uncomfortable emotional scenarios. Your biggest challenge is to tune in to your heart and communicate your feelings at the appropriate time of your own volition.

> **Key Words:** Protection, security, devotion, freedom, sanctuary, productivity, reclusion, withdrawal
>
> **Hermit Heart Positive:** I am dedicated to projects and loyal to very few people and to my pets.
>
> **Hermit Heart Negative:** I can withdraw completely when faced with uncomfortable displays of emotion.
>
> **Mantra:** I am keeping my heart open to mysterious feelings and practicing communication in my relationships.

The Rational Romantic

The Rational Romantic Heart Line, linked to the element Air, is long, flat, and straight, and ends in the lower quadrant formed by an imaginary cross below the index finger.

If you own this Heart Line, you are constantly assessing, analyzing, and pondering your own feelings and those of others. You loathe fights because disagreements give you even more to think, think, think about. Your thoughts swirl around you like the wind. One of your favorites songs might be "How Deep Is Your Love?" by the Bee Gees. Meaningful conversations, in which you have time to actually dialog with another person, are of utmost importance. Subtle nuances of words or facial expressions can put you into a tailspin of "What did she mean by *that?*" Your biggest challenge is to minimize your

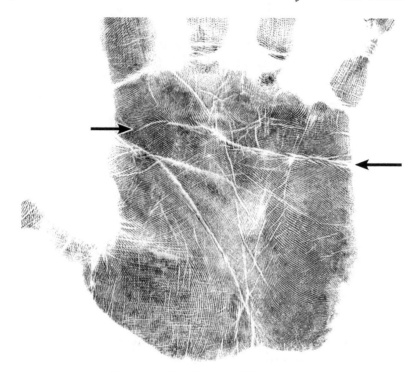

Figure 9: The Rational Romantic

own mental editing. Overly processing feelings come naturally to the Rational Romantic, and your best trait is consideration. It's very important for you to recognize and respect your own needs and desires and to make requests for those needs to be fulfilled.

> **Key Words:** Thoughtfulness, consideration, intellectuality, high-mindedness, meaning, examination, indecisiveness.
>
> **Rational Romantic Positive:** I am considerate and understanding of the thoughts and feelings of others.
>
> **Rational Romantic Negative:** I can lose myself in ideals and excessive analysis of others.
>
> **Mantra:** While I am appropriately mindful of the emotional needs of others, I am also aware of and honor my own passions.

Heart Line Impersonators

It is not uncommon to see a river veer off in another direction. People can be like that too. I consider an impersonator to be someone who subconsciously pretends to be someone he or she is not. Unfortunately, such a person can develop a deep, long-term pattern of revealing herself emotionally in ways other than that of her true type as shown in her Heart Line. It's not who she really is, and this, too, shows up in the palms.

A common impersonator is pictured in Figure 10. The curvature of this Heart Line would seem to end under the dotted arrow. However, at the last minute the actual Heart Line takes a sharp detour toward the index finger (under the solid arrow), signaling a Passionate Heart masquerading as a Big Heart.

Owners of Heart Lines that change course like this have easy access to two different Heart Line styles—think of a large tributary meeting the main river. Something within them flows in different directions. The owner of the hand in Figure 10 as a Passionate Heart is wired to be spontaneous, ask directly for what she wants, and display her vivaciousness without hesitation. However, as indicated by the

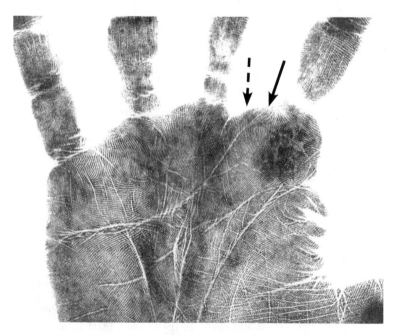

Figure 10: Passionate Heart impersonating a Big Heart

divergent line on her palm, her strong Big Heart tendencies typically dominate her emotional style, in which she is concerned about appearing selfish at the expense of others' feelings and desires. She might act to avoid the appearance of being manipulative to get her needs met. Her internal system is a bit confused as to which emotional style to claim.

After becoming aware of these Heart Line differences and understanding and claiming her real yet hidden Passionate Heart style, this woman said, "I always felt there was a big part of me that loved being spontaneous, the life of a party, needing to take care of my needs. Yet I felt compelled to be there for others in a big way. More times than not I would focus on the latter and get annoyed or resentful. Learning about the passionate part of myself has freed me to more regularly honor the passion in me and not feel guilty for being unable to be there for someone when it wasn't something I wanted to do from my heart or that I had the time to do."

Imagine the freedom she now feels. In a sense, she unmasked the impersonator to release and free herself so that she could see and be herself more clearly and authentically.

> **Key Words:** Enthusiastic, expressive, dramatic, suppressed spontaneity, disconnection, resentment

> **Passionate to Big Heart Positive:** I fully claim my natural style of spontaneous expression and release self-imposed obligation to meet the perceived needs of others.

> **Passionate to Big Heart Negative:** I am completely lost and annoyed with myself as I squelch my needs and wear this mask, with guilt.

> **Mantra:** In the moment, I recognize my true desires and make requests for what I want, while extending care and consideration for others, too.

Another possible Heart Line river system is one that splits into two or three forks. If all parts of the line still have the original width after the split, the owner will easily adapt to the Heart Line styles associated with each termination point.

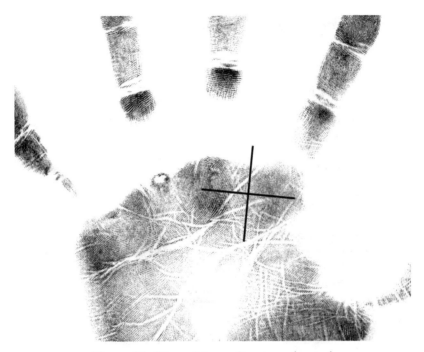

Figure 11: Heart Line splits near the end

In Figure 11 the main Heart Line splits under the middle finger into two forks. One fork curves up to the index finger, while the other runs straight, also ending under the index finger. In this case three different Heart Line descriptions apply: Hermit, where the split occurs, Big Heart, *and* Rational Romantic.

I call this configuration the Adaptable Affections Heart Line. If you see this configuration in your palm, you likely are considerate *and* cautious in your connections with others. As long as your non-negotiable need for freedom is recognized and protected, you will be balanced in thought, concern, and reflection in relationships, and you can adapt as required to the love style around you. If privacy, loyalty, and dependability are needed, with little effort you can cultivate your Hermit form. If a meaningful conversation is called for, you're all ears. You also have an innate knowledge of when a hug would be the perfect medicine. Because you can give up your private sanctuary as you over-adapt to the affectionate needs of others, your internal push–pull requires balancing between your need for alone time and social time.

Key Words: Adaptability, caution, consideration, helpfulness

Adaptable Affections Positive: I can put others first with a hug or conversation.

Adaptable Affections Negative: I give up my private sanctuary as I over-adapt to the needs of others.

Mantra: I am contemplating romance with a big heart without sacrificing my own heart center.

Heart Line Variations

The Heart Line can show a variety of interesting twists, turns, and formations. Sometimes certain lines will accompany the main Heart Line and reflect emotional subtleties of their owners. These arrangements are considered distractions to the main Heart Line type because they reduce the strength of the flow of the main river. It's important to recognize potential distractions in your emotional life so that you can make conscious choices for either self-acceptance or course-correction, as you desire. Let's take a look at a few variations.

Bending Over Backward

See the downward hook coming off the Heart Line in Figure 12 that resembles a miniature waterfall. This tiny deviation indicates that emotions of the heart are pouring out for another at the expense of the owner's emotional needs. Keeping the peace is a high priority to you if this is your Heart Line offshoot. Research has found owners of this marking have a serious inclination to rearrange their emotional response system to conform to the perceived wants of others. Saying "Yes" to go on a date when you don't really want to is something you might do if this formation is in your hand.

One client with this marking told me her "sympathy date" story. Her male friend hadn't had a date in two years. He had asked several women out, but no one would go with him. He even offered to pick them up and pay all expenses. Still no dates. After hearing his sad story, she told him she would go to a movie with him, in the hope of

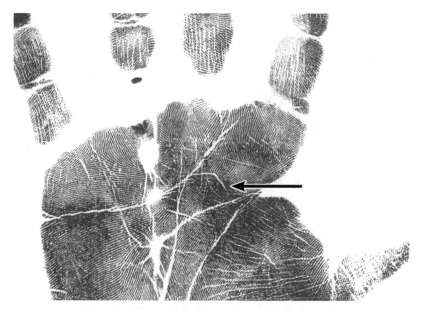

Figure 12: Bending Over Backward variation

lifting his spirits. He was elated. After the first movie, of course he asked her out again. Her intention was not to initiate a romantic relationship; it was simply a sympathetic reaction to his feelings. Instead of rejecting his invitation with a "No, thank you," she changed phone numbers and moved to a new location. She couldn't bear to hurt his feelings by telling him she didn't want to date him. She went from sympathy date to date escape.

Another client with the Bending Over Backward Line has repeatedly undermined her emotional power by taking in wounded souls. She has great sensitivity for lonely hearts. She stretches her empathy to excess, maintaining peace at any price, until she explodes. The explosion can happen internally or externally, or both. Inward explosions come with fear, guilt, self-criticism, and retreat. External outbursts create shame, self-doubt, and regret. In either case, the heart temporarily closes up. After I talked with her about an incident in which her relationship style had backfired, she realized clearly how she had plummeted over the raging waterfall—as the line suggests. Understanding the implications of this line and realizing how she was prone to rearrange her emotional behavior in the hope of a heartfelt outcome helped her regain control. Now she is more aware of the negative effects of too much sympathy and is claiming her emotional authority to refrain from excessive outpourings of the heart. The first step was awareness that she was giving away her power to nurture, protect, and avoid hurt feelings. The second step was not saying "yes" when the appropriate response was "no."

> **Key Words:** Empathy, understanding, sympathy, powerlessness, readjustment
>
> **Bending Over Backward Positive:** I care for and empathize deeply with the underdog.
>
> **Bending Over Backward Negative:** I can lose my emotional worth during self-obligated interactions with others.
>
> **Mantra:** By maintaining grace and respect for both others and myself, I am extending my heart appropriately.

Emotional Armor

Sometimes you'll find extra lines running parallel to the main Heart Line. These additional lines show extra channels where love has been intensely experienced, and also show a determination to protect the heart, like a suit of armor. If your hand shows such lines, you have a deep-seated need to keep your heart safe from being hurt. Pain is to be avoided at all cost. The extra parallel lines act as a shield and represent dependable protection to prevent rejection and disapproval. If you don't have this configuration but wish to better understand a friend who does, imagine a time in your life when your heart was broken. Was there a time in your life when your favorite pet died or had to be given away? Or imagine the heartache you felt as a result of your first break up in high school or college. The pain memory in the heart is so deep and the emotional loss so unbearable that a bulletproof vest is created around the heart to prevent that kind of pain from occurring again.

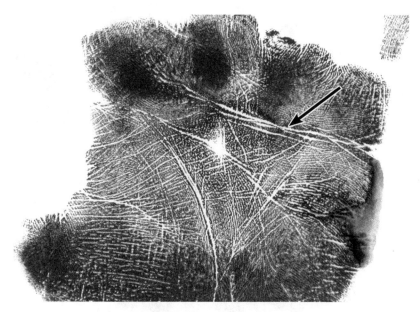

Figure 13: Emotional Armor variation

Key Words: Inner intensity, guardedness, vulnerability, choices

Emotional Armor Positive: I realize I am safe, and I move vulnerably into deep love at my own pace.

Emotional Armor Negative: I miss opportunities for deeper love.

Mantra: With conscious intention and courage, in full balance, I am appropriately opening to deeper levels of love.

Non-negotiable Love of Work

When you see the Fate Line starting near the bottom of the palm, climbing up to and merging with the Heart Line you'll find someone who is married to his or her career. I call this the Non-negotiable Love of Work Line.

If you find this arrangement on your own hands, you are comforted by an intense love of work and spend countless hours ambitiously

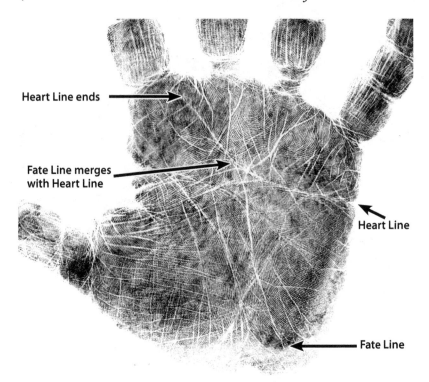

Heart Line ends

Fate Line merges
with Heart Line

Heart Line

Fate Line

Figure 14: Non-negotiable Love of Work variation

engaged in projects. Indulging in your ravenous love of effort makes you happy. Others may describe you as a workaholic and, yes, there is a strong tendency for extreme responsibility to tasks. Accomplishment is a value held near and dear to your heart. It's best to let those closest to you know not to interfere with your enthusiastic dedication for your career or projects. Letting them know of your delight in work will help them not to take your relationship aloofness personally. When I described this to a man with this design on his palm, he exclaimed, "I know! There are one hundred things I could be doing other than sitting here hearing about this."

> **Key Words:** Drive, intensity, focus, ambition, over-achievement, workaholism

> **Love of Work Positive:** I'm committed to getting it done with love and zeal!

Love of Work Negative: At what expense will I get it done? Is a personal relationship or my health being neglected at the expense of work?

Mantra: I am extending my love of work, projects, and tasks to key people in my life.

The Heart Line in Relationships

Now that you've learned your love style, you can better navigate your own river of love in relationships. Just knowing that everyone has his or her own love style helps because you can see how and why others behave in certain ways. Being aware of the characteristics of all four Heart Line types helps you more effectively relate to the people in your life. I've seen relationships go haywire when one person doesn't realize or acknowledge that another person has a different style of loving. I've heard clients say:

"Doesn't everyone feel like I do?"
"That's not how I'd express myself."
"Doesn't she care?"
"I do the yardwork every week, and I keep the cars maintained. Doesn't she realize I love her?"
"He needs my help; why isn't he accepting my invitation?"
"She is constantly texting me to find out where I am—all the time."
"I tend to process my feelings long after he is well on to his next adventure."

If you have felt this way, it might be that you've paired up with your opposite type, as it is natural to attract and align with the hearts of our opposites. To determine the opposites, look diagonally to the sections that are across from each other. Big Heart and Hermits are opposites, and Rational Romantics and Passionates are opposites.

Passionate		Big Heart	
Likes	Dislikes	Likes	Dislikes
Variety	Routine	Bonding	Disconnect
Banter	Restriction	Closeness	Curtness
Spontaneity	Wet blankets	Sharing	Withdrawal

Hermit		Rational Romantic	
Likes	Dislikes	Likes	Dislikes
Space	Clinginess	Consistency	Disagreement
Freedom	Demands	Consideration	Flippancy
Projects	Fickleness	Conversation	Drama

Notice how the emotional style and traits of each Heart Line type can attract or repel other Heart Line types. It's not uncommon to look to someone else to express a trait that you feel is lacking in yourself. The positive behavior of your opposite type will most likely be attractive to you, at first. Over time, however, the very qualities you initially adored can become irritating because they don't resonate with your own natural style of being, so it's natural to reject them. Perhaps self-criticizing thoughts exclaim, "I should be more like *that*." That kind of thinking adds fuel to the fire of irritation. The remedy is to let go of judgments and accept emotional behaviors that are unlike yours.

In this way, your opposite type opens you up to an expanded version of yourself. For example, the Hermit is comfortable spending time alone working on projects. The advanced Hermit has learned to keep her heart open, be drawn to the Big Heart (her opposite type), and connect with her partner through heartfelt communication, although she might initiate such communication less frequently than the Big Heart. Conversely, for the Big Heart it's important to care and nurture, as she loves to do, while also keeping attuned to her center, like the Hermit. However, the Big Heart will appear clingy to the Hermit, and the Hermit will appear heartless to the Big Heart. The Passionate opens up to her opposite by being her naturally dynamic self and making her wants known, while also considering the needs of her partner—a little bit. The Rational Romantic will advance as she considers the needs and emotions of another while sometimes also identifying her own desires, like the Passionate. However, there will be many times when the Passionate appears flippant to the Rational Romantic and the Rational Romantic will appear detail-oriented to the Passionate.

Of course, you're more than your Heart Line type. But you can see how these emotional differences can interfere with expectations in relationship.

Complications will arise if you are not true to your Heart Line type. Consider the ramifications of changing the flow of the river. What would it take for the Amazon or the Ganges River to change course? It would require colossal landscape changes. Likewise, if you begin acting like a different Heart Line type, trouble will certainly ensue. When starting a relationship, you can suffer from heart-language amnesia. This means you can conform to some ideal you think the other person would like to see in you and forget your true heart language. This state of amnesia is dangerous because it's short lived and the real emotional style will eventually come forward. It's essential, therefore, to live in the real emotional style from day one with any prospective partner.

See how understanding your natural emotional flow and purposely aligning with it can help you improve your relationships. Consider how embracing and integrating the characteristics of your opposite, just a little bit, might help you advance on your love path. Now ponder how your acceptance of others' emotional styles will benefit both you and them. Consider how another person's emotional style is simply his or her way of being. At the beginning of this discussion I asked you to imagine improving your relationships by ten percent. With this new awareness of your own and of opposing emotional styles, you can increase that percentage even further and master your relationships—starting today. Imagine how your mate might respond!

Your Assignment for Deeper Discovery

1. Using the words in the book, describe some of the key words and the positive and negative interpretations of your Heart Lines. (*See the example on the following page.*)

Page: _____

Right hand key words:

_____

_____

Right hand positive interpretation:

_____

_____

Right hand negative interpretation:

_____

_____

Left hand key words:

_____

_____

Left hand positive interpretation:

_____

_____

Left hand negative interpretation:

_____

_____

Example

1. Using the words in the book, describe some of the key words and the positive and negative interpretations of your Heart Lines.

Page: __36-37__

Right hand key words:
   __Hermit Heart Line. Need space, freedom, and sanctuary__

Right hand positive interpretation:
   __Dedicated to projects__

Right hand negative interpretation:
   __Withdraw when faced with emotions__

---

2. If what you've written in the chart describes you, transcribe it into your "My Hand Analysis Blending Guide" assignment at the back of the book, and include the mantra for your Heart Line type(s).

3. The Head Line

Understanding Your Essential Mental Tendencies

"We are what we think. All that we
are arises with our thoughts. With
our thoughts we make the world."
—*Guatama Buddha*

THE HEAD LINE in your hands represents the unique operation of your mental system. Just as your computer has a central processing unit, you do too. The Head Line, associated with the element Air, starts on the inside of the palm, on the thumb side of the hand, and travels toward the outer edge of the hand. Consider what happens in the air around you: information flows. As invisible radio signals travel through the air, so too do your ideas, thoughts, concepts, theories, and perceptions surge though your internal airways. These channels are your mental wiring system. Nature has created an etching in your hand to depict how your unique computer system is programmed. How you plan, calculate, analyze, estimate, and integrate ideas can be read from this major line in your hands. In short, the Head Line is examined to understand the thinking system of its owner.

The Head Line is different on every hand. Head Lines range in length from short to very long. Their shape can be straight and flat, rounded downward, or deeply curving toward the wrist. Origination points must also be considered. Is the beginning of the Head Line attached to the Life Line, or separated from the Life Line? Check the quality of the line. Is it clear and flowing smoothly? If so, it indicates clear thinking. Does it break, then restart at a new point? If so, its owner's mental computer is liable to flip off line and reboot every now and then. Is the course of the Head Line wavy, jagged, messy, or cluttered with braids or bubbles? If so, its owner needs more time to process information. This may include asking others to be patient while taking time to contemplate, focus, and make decisions.

If you experience frequent confusion in your thinking, it will show up in your hands. And as you resolve the stresses causing the confusion, your Head Line will reflect your new sense of clarity. These are just a few of the possibilities for Head Line designs.

Everyone comprehends information differently; people think and make decisions in different ways. Understanding your own method of decision-making and then considering another's different method can generate patience and compassion when relating to one another.

In the following pages we will examine these features of the Head Line:

- Length: short, medium, long, very long
- Shape: straight, downward curving, curving deeply downward toward the wrist, flipping upward at the end
- Origination point: joined together with or separated from the Life Line, curves down from index finger
- Quality: clear, jagged or messy, broken
- Configuration: union with the Heart Line, X on the end, forking at the end
- Color: pink, red, blue, yellow, white

Head Line Length

The shorter the Head Line, the less time the owner spends computing. If the short line is clear, its owner is not likely to change his or her mind after making a decision, and will probably give you quick answers. A Head Line is considered short when it extends about one and one-half inches from the thumb side of the palm, as shown in Figure 15.

For example, one of my clients, who has a short- to medium-length Head Line, bought shares in a very successful stock and explained to me how she decided to buy that stock: "I just did!" She received a tip from a friend, liked the product, and just thought she was in the right place at the right time.

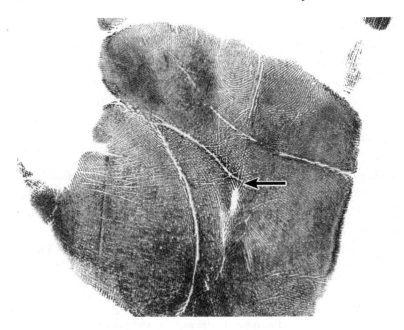

Figure 15: Short Head Line

Conversely, the longer the line, the more time is spent "online" considering and compartmentalizing information and problems. If you ask a person with a long, straight, horizontal Head Line how she chose the car she bought, she might reply, "I did extensive research with Consumer Reports. I assessed dependability, options, and crash test statistics, then compared prices of similar vehicles. I considered down payment options and payment plans. After a thorough analysis, I made the purchase."

The Super Synthesizer

When the Head Line is clear, extends with consistent thickness straight across the hand, as if it were drawn in with a pen, and terminates about one-quarter to one-half inch before the edge of the palm, you'll find a Super Synthesizer. This person won't feel fulfilled unless she has an avenue in which to use her multifaceted system of comprehension and analysis. Think of this very long Head Line acting like an eight-armed octopus that must be in full synthesis mode in order to feel a deep sense of satisfaction. Each of the eight arms is equipped with numerous sense-gathering suction cups, too.

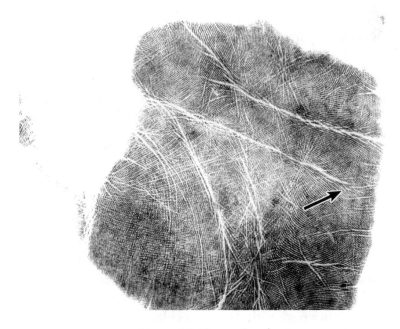

Figure 16: Super Synthesizer

Richard Unger calls such a long, clear Head Line HAL 9000, after the supercomputer in the science fiction story *2001: A Space Odyssey*. I relay Unger's description to my clients and watch their eyes open wide. In unison their body language matches their voice, saying, "Oh yes, that's me."

The following is the description I give to my long Head Lined clients and students. In *2001: A Space Odyssey*, HAL is the central processing unit that controls everything on an entire Pan Am spaceship on a secret mission from Earth to Jupiter. HAL was the brain and nervous system of the ship and reported all problems to mission control.

HAL was constantly occupied, and said, "I find things difficult to put out of my mind." This is the gift and the curse of the octopus brain. On a good day, he put many things together in an orderly fashion. On a bad day, he gets into a tangle.

In the end, having a bad day, HAL went haywire. He no longer had big enough problems to solve, so he over-analyzed little problems. The same can be said for someone with a HAL 9000 Head Line when not engaged in big challenging problems—the more complicated, the better. Assembling scraps of fabric for an elaborate quilt or reorganizing an entire corporation may suit Mr. or Ms. HAL, depending on other features in the hands. The Super Synthesizer Head Line has definite mental requirements—large, important projects with massive amounts of data.

Children with long Head Lines need enough intellectual challenge from school and home projects to keep them busy, otherwise they may very well create problems with siblings, friends, or schoolmates.

Once a father brought his eight-year-old daughter to me for a reading. She had a very long and clear Head Line. After I described her talent as a "super-duper computer," she told me that she was very good at math and loved it. Unfortunately, she was teased by some of her classmates for having an advanced aptitude in mathematics. I encouraged her to maintain true friendships with those who would value her mental gifts.

If you are the owner of a Super Synthesizing Head Line, a sure sign that you're not using your full potential is relationship problems. By initiating problems in relationships with others, you give yourself juicy problems to wrestle with. This makes HAL very happy, in a computer kind of way.

Key Words: Complexity, synthesis, amalgamation, analysis, boredom

Super Synthesizer Positive: I use my exceptional mental aptitude to fully engage in colossal complexity, synthesizing large amounts of information.

Super Synthesizer Negative: Without enough data to manipulate, I instigate big problems to solve, usually in relationships.

Mantra: I exercise my ability to engage in the complex synthesis of thoughts without creating tangled webs within my closest relationships.

Head Line Shape

The Guide for Lost Souls

The shape of the Head Line reveals the nature of a person's mind. Straight Head Lines belong to people who are logical, rational, and practical thinkers. Downward curving Head Lines, as in Figure 17, belong to individuals who are creative and reflective, with imaginative flair. If the line curves deeply into the lower part of the palm, you'll find someone with a natural capacity for diving into deep emotional waters with compassion, sensitivity, and even sadness.

The owner of a long Head Line that curves deep into the palm considers ideas, thoughts, and activities that are influenced by deep meaning in life. People with Head Lines resembling Figure 18 have felt the trap that Persephone felt after Hades kidnapped her to make her his wife. Held against her will, Persephone was trapped in the dark, dismal, gloomy underworld. If you have this deeply curving Head Line, you most likely understand the feeling of depression. It doesn't

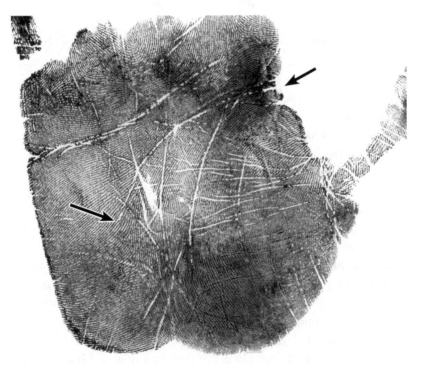

Figure 17: Downward Curving—creative and imaginative

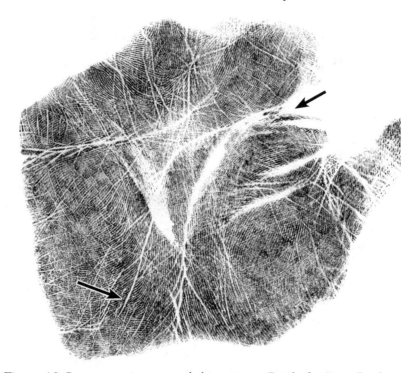

Figure 18: Long, curving toward the wrist—Guide for Lost Souls

mean you are depressed but you know what it means to be depressed. Like Persephone, you have experienced despair associated with "your life not being your own." You are sensitive and responsive to your environment, including the feelings of all beings. As Persephone matured she opened her heart to Hades *and* to the other lost souls ensnared in the underworld. Likewise, as you mature you develop a deep compassion for others that can develop into life work as a guide for people who have been led astray or trapped. A deeply curving Head Line represents a potential path to mature into the Queen of the Underworld, handling hidden and all-consuming emotion, where reason has no place. Persephone also knew that she would return to the bright world above in spring each year. You have a genius for understanding others who enter into their own world of deep and unpredictable waters.

After describing the implication of this type of Head Line to one client, she confirmed the analysis saying, "Oh, yes, that's me. Unexpectedly, I dive into a very dark place. I'm used to it now, so I have a minifridge in my room with ice cream in it. I comfort myself on my favorite fluffy bedspread with DVDs next to my TV. I do know I'll eventually resurface to everyday life." Persephone did resurface out of the darkness, after choosing to do so, and realized her power in the decision and in her journey.

> **Key Words:** Despair, grief, powerlessness, empathy, resurrection
>
> **Guide for Lost Souls Positive:** I am able to be fully and completely present with deep sadness, maintain compassion, and steer others to their inner light.
>
> **Guide for Lost Souls Negative:** Immobile, I remain a victim of kidnapping by hopelessness, believing I have no way out.
>
> **Mantra:** I willingly open myself to deep emotion and am appropriately available to myself and other lost souls ready to "come back to life," again, feeling joy.

One of my clients has a different Head Line on each hand. The Head Line on her right hand dives deeply into the bottom of her palm toward her wrist, like Figure 18. On her left hand she has a very long Head Line, like the Super Synthesizer (Figure 16). After she heard about the descriptions of these two lines and their owners' thinking systems, she said, "I felt an overwhelming sense of connectedness with my life. I realized I was both able to go deep into a mood *and* to make sense of the information afterwards. I activate both mental systems: one for going into the deep waters, and one to analyze and resolve complicated problems after I return to the surface."

Bottom Line Mind

When a Head Line travels across the palm on a steady course, then flips upward at the end, its owner may have an uncontrollable urge to get to the bottom line and speak his or her truth. It's as if the pinkie finger is invisibly pulling the end of the Head Line upward.

This long Head Line indicates a super processor with the ability to dart to the bottom line at lightning speed. This person is aware of

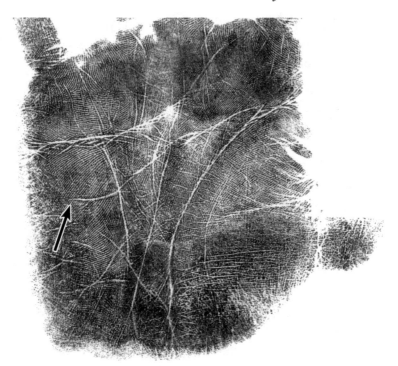

Figure 19: The Bottom Line Mind

what is really going on behind the scenes. She can condense a two-hour movie into two sentences. The author of the CliffsNotes who summarized the literary work of *War and Peace* probably had the Bottom Line Mind Head Line configuration.

One owner of this line configuration told me, "It can be very painful to listen to someone drag out a story or an explanation when I already know where it's going. I've learned how crucial it is to be patient and to bite my tongue so that others can finish speaking."

It's important for the person with this marking to find an approving audience for his agile, extra-aware, no-nonsense mind, otherwise he may be considered ruthless. When someone is wired for getting to the bottom line and telling it like it is spontaneously, he can appear quite insensitive. Friends and family may not have praised his urge to "get to the point" or his skill in doing so. The best remedy for such a person is to have an outlet in which he can be fully engaged in truth-telling, while being in an arena where he is accepted and acknowledged for that skill.

Key Words: Alertness, shrewdness, astuteness, callousness

Bottom Line Mind Positive: Count on me for the truth without fluff.

Bottom Line Mind Negative: Without being tactful, my sharp, bottom line mind can alienate friends and family or, worse, I'll stuff it all in self-condemnation.

Mantra: With grace and diplomacy I use my laser-sharp mind effectively in a setting where I am received.

Origination Point

The Advocate Head Line

This Head Line originates inside and below the initiation of the Life Line, just above the inset of the thumb. This is considered the Mars Mount. If you have this configuration you're watchful and mentally alert. You can be headstrong about seeing both sides of the same coin. You're a determined debater, but you can seem argumentative to someone not interested in debate.

One child I read for who had this marking kept answering my questions with other questions. It was hard to get anywhere with his quarrelsome character. You see, the Head Line, which represents the mental system, is dipping into the Mars Mount. Mars is a protector, capable of combat for his or her cause. The mental processor is fed by the courage and bravery of Mars, the warrior.

The owner of the Advocate Head Line typically guards his or her thoughts, keeping them ready, in a sense, to defend his or her cause. He or she can be seen as prudish when his or her thoughts and resulting words contradict others. It might seem that this person is narrow-minded, but in actuality he or she thrives when seeing differently. Such a person makes an excellent social or political activist, waging war for the underdog.

The late UCLA basketball coach John Wooden did not want "yes-men" around him. He encouraged his assistant coaches to argue

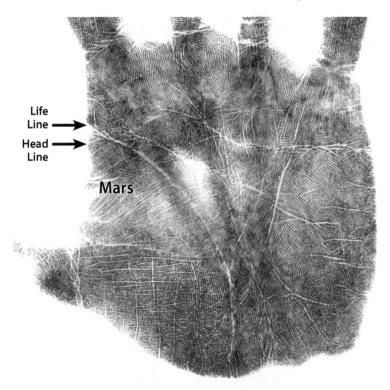

Figure 20: The Advocate

their points of view with him. He, in turn, responded strongly with his own opinions. Gary Cunningham, one of his head coaches said, "This was Coach Wooden's way of testing how much the assistant coaches believed in what they were telling him and how much they knew about the points they were advocating." But Coach Wooden also knew that it is difficult to effect positive change when you antagonize others. "The purpose of criticism is to correct, improve, and change; rarely to humiliate or embarrass," he said. I didn't see Coach Wooden's hands, but I wouldn't be surprised if he had the Advocate Head Line configuration. He was also a high-profile crusader helping people to be their personal best.

Key Words: Cautiousness, watchfulness, debate, prudence, argumentativeness

The Advocate Positive: I am steadfast in considering

contrary viewpoints and contribute many perspectives to uphold the conversation.

The Advocate Negative: If no one else can ever win, and I'm seen as an antagonist, I can become a loner by exclusion.

Mantra: For the cause, I use my skills of assertive thinking in tactful, savvy ways.

Independence

If the start of the Head Line is separated from the beginning of the Life Line, the owner's thought system will be independent of his or her family of origin, acting autonomously.

If you have this marking of self-reliance, you prefer to figure things

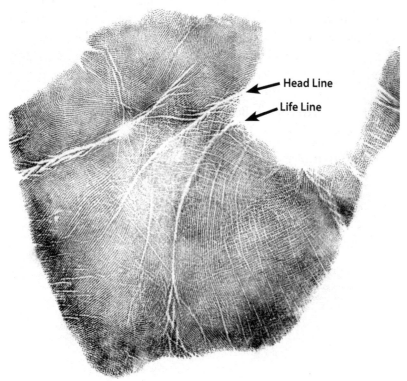

Figure 21: Independence

out on your own. For example, if you must decide whether to get married or divorced, go to college or quit college, start a job or change vocations, you rely on the resources of your own choosing, which may not include family or tribal input.

I initiated Project Snowflake in early 2010 to observe changes in twelve children's handprints over the course of ten years. The starting age of the participants ranged from five days to eight years of age. The handprint in Figure 21 belongs to one of the children in Project Snowflake. At the time of this printing she was fifteen years of age. As a youngster, her mental system did not match those of her parents as closely as one might think, even though they lived in a loving and supportive country home environment. She showed signs of operating on her own terms as early as age three. I first printed her hands when she was eight years old before I started the project; she is now eighteen. All of her handprints, spanning ten years, clearly show her tendency toward independence, freedom, and autonomy. She did her own thing on the soccer field in the sixth grade, not paying much attention to the position to which she had been assigned. At age fourteen, she snuck out of her bedroom in the middle of the night to meet her friends in the schoolyard. As soon as she could, she eagerly moved out of her parents' home to work and attend college.

Key Words: Self-sufficiency, autonomy, self-governance, freedom

Independence Positive: I have a large capacity to get the job done, especially when unsupervised.

Independence Negative: I don't see the need for help very often, and this can make it challenging to team up with others toward a common goal.

Mantra: I relish my independent mind, but I am open to receiving support from the team once in a while.

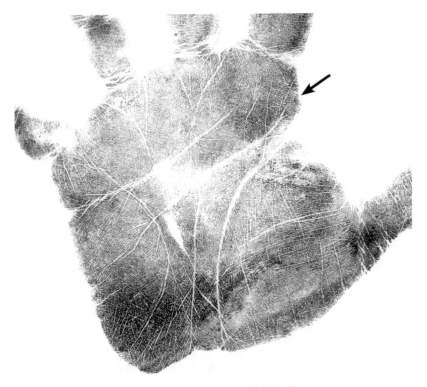

Figure 22: Motivated Mind

Motivated Mind

If the Head Line starts with an arc coming down from the index finger, its owner is motivated to formulate action plans based on high ideals, visions, and dreams. The line acts like an antenna, downloading inspiration and strategies to the leader within. The owner of such a Head Line is capable of brilliant influence through a continual flow of ideas for the betterment of the territory in which she resides (or reigns). She is inclined to fuel other people's ideas and plans, in the form of solutions.

> **Key Words:** Strategy, stimulation, solutions, action, confidence, inspiration

> **Motivated Mind Positive:** I inspire and offer solutions with a high level of confidence.

Motivated Mind Negative: I lack emotional sensitivity when I'm in my solutions-only brain.

Mantra: I offer my brilliant solutions with discernment and implement them with consideration.

Family Influence

When the Head and Life lines are entwined at their starting point above the inset of the thumb, you'll find that family is a strong consideration in the owner's mental makeup. It's more common than not to see the Head and Life lines of both hands connected for at least a half inch as they begin. The longer the Head and Life lines connect, the stronger the dependence on the family of origin. Even if the owner

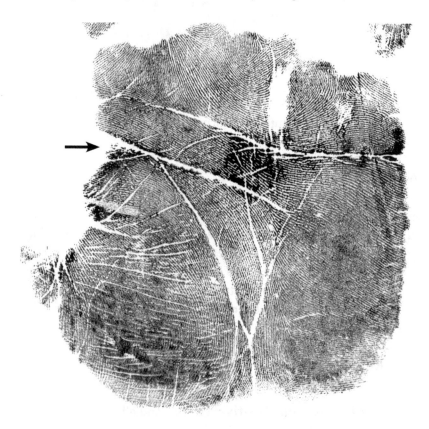

Figure 23: Family Influence

doesn't live near his or her family, there is a dependence on family and community influence.

One of my client's Head and Life lines entwine for about an inch on both hands. His family (brother, two sisters, and mother) share a home that they all purchased together. The family works together in business as artists, musicians, and Flamenco dancers. It's common to see the entire family together at a coffee shop.

You might see this configuration on a person's right hand but not the left hand, or vice versa. If the right hand is stamped with Family Influence, but not the left, that person will be perceived as a team player by the outside world. When it's on the left hand but not the right, read it as described above.

I have not given positive–negative interpretations for Family Influence because it's one of the most natural configurations in the palm.

Qualities

Broken Head Line

Breaks in the Head Line represent glitches in the data-processing department. Thoughts and speech will flow for a while, but all of a sudden the system goes on pause. A mini-reboot is needed when the Head Line is broken. Not to fear, the system will restart and thoughts, ideas, and speech will continue. If you find a Head Line that is broken, look to see which finger the line is broken under; the energy associated with that finger will influence the disruption in the thinking system. For example, if the Head Line is broken under the middle finger, its owner might find herself stumped by responsibility or money issues. If the Head Line is broken under the ring finger, its owner might freeze with fright at the prospect of being on stage, or might stifle her creative expression to protect herself against rejection. (We'll learn more about the fingers in Chapter 6.)

I've seen Head Lines break and reconnect. An eight-year-old in my Project Snowflake had a hand with a broken Head Line. The break was only for a fraction of an inch, and the line resumed and continued toward the edge of the hand. When I asked his family how he spoke when telling of something like scoring a goal in a soccer game, his sister told me that he would sometimes stop talking in midstream.

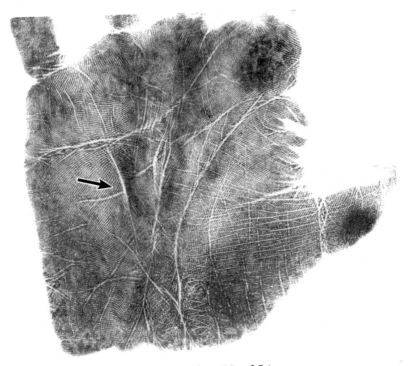

Figure 24: Broken Head Line

I asked her not to complete his sentences for him anymore, knowing that he'd get back "online" and complete his thought on his own. He's now twelve years old, and his Head Line is continuous.

One woman with a broken Head Line was sixty-five years old when she first came to see me. She was going through a divorce from her husband. The situation was very messy and very difficult financially. Real estate, money, and other assets were up in the air. The attorney was getting nowhere fast. The woman was paralyzed with worry. In three different readings over two years, we watched her Head Line change from attached to broken, then become attached again. Reattachment occurred after the divorce and all associated issues were resolved. (Note that while this woman's Head Line behaved according to the circumstances of her life, it does not mean anyone else's Head Line will respond in the same way.)

If you hear someone say, on a somewhat regular basis, "Oh, I just lost my thought" or "I lost my head," or if a person changes topics in midstream, check the Head Line to see if is broken or jagged. As you do, see the correlation between the Head Line on the hand and the thought system in the head.

> **Key Words:** Intermittence, hesitation, uncertainty, delay, reboot, restart

> **Broken Head Line Positive:** I have a thought about this, now give me a second to reboot and resume my mental processing.

> **Broken Head Line Negative:** It seems as though others continually complete my thoughts or sentences for me.

> **Mantra:** I am patient with myself and politely ask others to allow me to finish my thought without interrupting me.

Split Thinking

It is not uncommon to see the Head Line split into two or even three lines at the end.

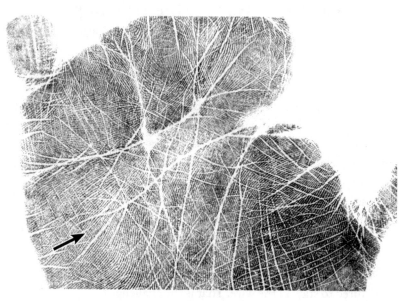

Figure 25: Split Thinking

When a Head Line forks into two or three lines that continue for a half-inch or more, its owner will quickly move from one line of thought to another. If this is your Head Line you may feel split in your thinking on various topics. For example, you might be thinking about getting your kids to school, attending a teacher-parent conference, *and* your next business proposal—all at once!

> **Key Words:** Diversity, discrepancy, distraction
>
> **Split Thinking Positive:** I am able to think and speak on one track, then jump gracefully to another track, according to the situation I'm in.
>
> **Split Thinking Negative:** I become distracted by multiple directions of thought.
>
> **Mantra:** I appreciate my ability to travel down diverse lines of thought, and I use this capacity wisely.

Configuration

The Simian Line—Walking the Tight Rope

Sometimes the Head and Heart Lines are fused together into one channel. If you see one straight line crossing the entire hand and you can't see both a Head and a Heart Line, you've found a Simian Line.

This line acts as a divide separating the upper and the lower areas of the hand. The divide resembles a tight rope. Walking a tight rope takes extreme balance, focus, training, skill, and courage. The documentary film *Man on Wire* depicts the dogged drive, internal discipline, and relentless engagement needed to walk a tight rope. The film includes home movies showing the walker in training as a young boy: nothing seems to matter except walking the wire. The documentary climaxes when he attains his lifelong dream of walking a wire between the twin towers of the World Trade Center in New York.

Now imagine walking on a high wire while it is being pulled in opposite directions, like the rope in tug-of-war. Even more focus would be required to stay on the wire. That is the challenge facing people with Simian Lines. You may find yourself walking quickly, if not sprinting,

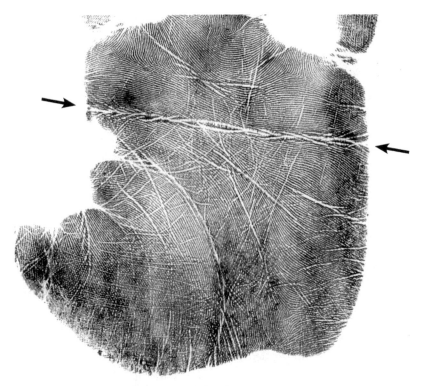

Figure 26: The Simian Line

back and forth between opposites. You may notice that others do not operate with the level of passion and intensity you have. Conversely, others may not understand why you are so concentrated on the task of the moment. There is nothing wrong with you. You simply have tremendous ability and energy. You are learning to harness and apply that power effectively.

One Simian Line owner told me about the time she decided to replace the carpet in her living room with wood flooring. Once she made up her mind, the carpet was ripped out within twenty-four hours. Within the next twenty-four hours the wood flooring was purchased and installation had begun! Those around her mostly watched. Another woman with a Simian Line, a professional weaver, asked her roommates not to disturb her and not to take it personally if she didn't respond to them when she was weaving for hours on end.

If you wear this special line, you engage life at an extremely high level of intensity. You approach projects, work, and relationships with penetrating concentration. You may feel challenged to communicate effectively; the thinking system (head) is tightly interwoven with your feelings system (heart), and therefore influences how the words flow out of your mouth. You may think you are being very clear with another person, but they just don't seem to get what you're saying. This causes you to feel misunderstood. Likewise, words coming to you from another person may become garbled or may be misinterpreted. This can be frustrating for both parties. Your job is to stick with it: keep articulating your thoughts as best as you can, with heart. You are on the path to communications mastery.

Allow yourself to act, react, and retreat, and accept yourself in doing so. Although you think and feel deeply, you believe others don't sense that about you. As you "over-process" on the inside, others may see you as either a runaway freight train, or aloof and uncaring. Your job is to communicate in a variety of ways so that you will be understood. Practice, practice, practice! Give yourself time to percolate those intense feeling-thoughts. Clarify your desires. For more insight on the Simian Line, return to the chapter on Heart Lines and read about both the Hermit and the Rational Romantic, because the Simian Line contains both of those Heart Lines. To release interior tension, engage in physical activities such as running, racquetball, kayaking, or yoga. As you embrace the unity of your heartfelt mental processing unit, you will be transported to new levels on your personal evolutionary journey.

> **Key Words:** Communications, intensity, concentration, focus, misunderstandings
>
> **Simian Line Positive:** Excellence in communication results from my persistence and determination.
>
> **Simian Line Negative:** Continual misunderstandings make me retreat into a voiceless life.
>
> **Mantra:** With vigor and drive I gracefully walk the tightrope, honoring my true desires and aiming for and claiming communications mastery.

Desire Confusion

In this configuration the vertical Mercury Line and a third line cross the Head Line. The intersection creates the appearance of a star.

Owners of this marking agree one hundred percent of the time when I suggest that they have lost their own desires for the sake of someone else's. While doing a five-minute reading for a classmate as part of my master's degree presentation at the University of Santa Monica, this marking on her palm jumped out at me. It was as though no other markings existed on her hands. I suggested that she was inclined to take on the dream of another, and in so doing to be completely detached from her own desires. She exclaimed, "Oh, that is so me! My year-long project was my late husband's aspiration, not mine. He is the one who absolutely loved the project I completed—I didn't." She wasn't disappointed in her decision; in a sense, he lived on as she completed the project.

Another woman I read for took up her fiancé's favorite sport, even though it wasn't something she was truly passionate about. After fifteen years of marriage she still engages in his passion. Yes, she enjoys it, but it's not hers.

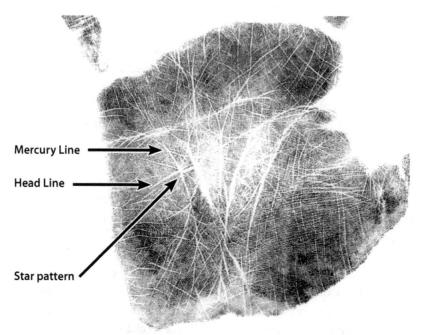

Figure 27: Desire Confusion

When I see this marking I recommend that its owner start a journal to identify his or her desires and the choices that he or she makes each day, so that the personal desire system can be developed. The journal should also include what the person *doesn't* want, so that those activities can be released. The aim is for the person to become aware of his or her true desires and to find appropriate ways to fulfill them without guilt.

> **Key Words:** Codependency, numbness, frustration, guilt
>
> **Desire Confusion Positive:** I focus with consideration as I adopt another person's dreams and desires, while developing the muscle for my own.
>
> **Desire Confusion Negative:** My desire system is broken. I don't know what I want.
>
> **Mantra:** I am conscious of the desires I have subscribed to and know that I am able to design my own life dream in the way that I want.

Color of the Head Line

The color of your Head Line changes based on the circumstance you're in. Regardless of nationality, a red line indicates angry thoughts, blue indicates sorrow, yellow shows critical thinking, pink is normal, and white indicates a shortage of mental power.

In summary, you should try to understand your mental tendencies and thought patterns so that your internal central processing unit can be appropriately engaged. If you have a capacity for certain types of mental processing and that capacity is not being fully used or appreciated, take steps to find an ideal environment where it will.

Mental routines, represented by your Head Line, are not permanent. Habits can be changed, but awareness, willingness, and effort are required. You can overcome confusion, uncertainty, disorder, or fear. The first step is to recognize that you'd like to change something and think differently. The next step is to invoke discipline for change. You *can* do more than you think!

No Head Line is better than another. Use the Head Line you have to the best of your ability. Ideally, you are already in the right setting to take advantage of your mental processing attributes. For example, the quick decisions of a person with a short Head Line would work well in a hospital emergency room. A long Head Line Super Synthesizer would flourish when setting up and running a nationwide chain of children's daycare centers.

Of course, these simple suggestions do not take into consideration other markings in the hand that would indicate more precisely the best direction to take. Blending the markings in your hands is crucial for getting a whole picture. Take a moment now to take note of the Head Line type you have on each hand, and complete the assignment on the following page. Remember, the Head Line on your dominant hand, which is usually the right hand, will show how you process your thoughts in the outer world—in public. The Head Line on your non-dominant hand, which is usually the left hand, will show how you process your thoughts in the inner world—when in private.

Your Assignment for Deeper Discovery

1. Using the words in the book, describe some of the key words and the positive and negative interpretations of your Head Lines. (*See the example on the following page.*)

Page: _____

Right hand key words:

_____

_____

Right hand positive interpretation:

_____

_____

Right hand negative interpretation:

_____

_____

Left hand key words:

_____

_____

Left hand positive interpretation:

_____

_____

Left hand negative interpretation:

_____

_____

Example

1. Using the words in the book, describe some of the key words and the positive and negative interpretations of your Head Lines.

Page: __56__

Right hand key words:

   Super Synthesizer Head Line, synthesizer, need
   complicated problems to solve

Right hand positive interpretation:

   Exceptional mental capacity

Right hand negative interpretation:

   I can create problems in relationship so I'll have
   something to solve

2. If what you've written in the chart describes you, transcribe it into your "My Hand Analysis Blending Guide" assignment at the back of the book, and include the mantra for your Head Line type(s).

4. The Life Line

Decipher Your Vitality System and Live in Balance

> *"Riches are not from abundance, but*
> *from a contented mind."*
>
> —*Lao Tzu*

THE LIFE LINE is a major line that is carved on the inside of the hand around the Venus Mount at the base of the Thumb. The length, shape, and quality of the Life Line are associated with the state of the physical body, and with awareness of and attention to the physical world. Let me put one myth to rest: the length of the Life Line does *not* predict the length of one's life. It does, however, show concerns about protection and preservation of the body. The Life Line is also called the Line of Earth. It is considered the line of family and tribe because we build our physical constitutions within our tribes. As humans, we look to our communities for support and safety. If we feel safe in our clans, our core energy systems are more likely to be in balance.

The Life Line can be read for personal vitality, productivity, stability and energy management, physical strength and stamina, and relationship to the sense of physical safety. Someone with a long, clear, and deep Life Line is down to earth, with a strong sense of security and stamina for living. Conversely, someone with a short or weak Life Line will feel constantly restless, a bit edgy, and will have a tendency to "fly." Such a person may be living on the surface of life, staying busy but not really "digging in."

Long Life Line on One Who Died Young

Figure 28 shows proof that the length of the Life Line does not indicate the length of life. This client died around age fifty-five. Her Life Line was long, well carved, and without damage or weakness of any kind, and the round curvature of the line shows robustness. When I printed her hands in 2005 she was healthy, active, enthusiastic, fully engaged with life, and quite bubbly. Later that year she entered the hospital for stomach pains. She was kept in the hospital for further testing and was soon diagnosed with an inoperable tumor in her stomach. She died within two weeks.

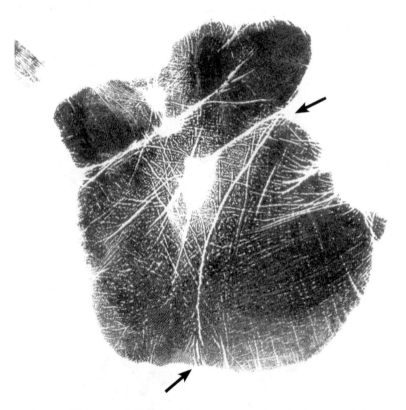

Figure 28: Long Life Line on a woman who died at age fifty-five

Types of Life Line

Short, Weak, or Broken Life Line

If your Life Line is short, delicate, or scattered, you have difficulty resting. Your personal anchor and grounding system has been compromised. Because you're accustomed to living in a routine of "flight," you may not recognize these patterns as you read about them for the first time. For example, your work or family life may involve your driving from one place to another and another. You might feel as though you're constantly scrambling to get your life in order. You may think, "There's not enough time to get it all done!" Core survival issues, such as paying the rent, keeping your job, and having enough food, remain strong considerations in your life and family. At worst, a sense of support from family is severely lacking, which creates a lack of trust in the tribal system. If your tribal system is at risk, you are more likely to

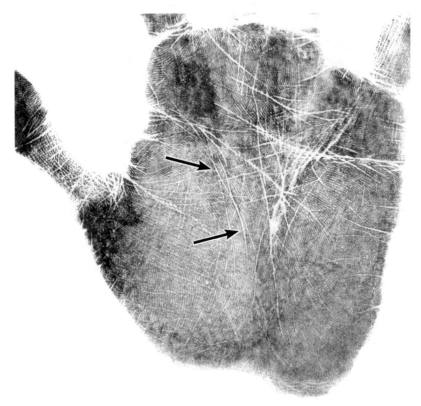

Figure 29: Scattered and reluctant to rest

doubt your role and value in society, asking, "Do I belong here?" Doubt of one's role in the community can cause anxiety and internal tension that, in turn, produce a strong urge to create safety for oneself and others. When this is recognized and more clearly understood, one can begin to implement change, increasing stability instead of insecurity. If you have this type of Life Line, create and implement a plan for poise, routine, and balance on a regular basis.

After I consulted with the woman whose hand is shown in Figure 29, she shared the following with me:

My Search for Survival

I loved my childhood. It was wonderful until my mother became ill. By the time I was fifteen, I was taking care of my mother, my three younger siblings, and myself, as well as going to school and managing the household. This is when the feeling of "running" started.

I lived at home until my mother passed on. I was twenty-three at that time. I knew that if I was to have my own life, now was the time to move, and I needed to move as far away from my dad and younger siblings as I could. So I moved across the country.

Far away from immediate family, I searched for a new family and community. After several years of searching, I took a job with a corporation that had the culture of a large family. After being there two years I married, but I continued to have the feeling of running, as I was so used to that pattern. It took many years of being with the same company and spouse before the feeling of running started to subside.

This woman built a life around her job in a corporate family, and with her husband of seventeen years, to help soothe her urge to flight just enough to let her feel safe and more or less grounded. The owner of a short or weak Life Line will feel lost if he or she is not busy doing something—all of the time. It's natural for such a person to create security through work to feel safe.

If you have a short or weak Life Line and would like to cultivate more stability and peace in your life, take time to sit still long enough to realize that you *are* actually safe in your body. Consider implementing a regular breathing practice so that you can truly feel the harmony and tranquility you are seeking.

A broken Life Line indicates a very difficult circumstance, usually involving a serious injury such as a head trauma, a life-changing event such as divorce, moving to another state, or death in the family. Events associated with a broken Life Line can be seen in a positive or negative way, but either way a broken Life Line probably represents a needed wake-up call. For example, one man with a break in his Life Line had very destructive behaviors, such that his wife divorced him and took custody of their children. He saw the separation in a negative way, but the divorce helped him to realize that he would benefit by making positive changes for healthier behaviors.

In my observations and in the life histories of my clients, issues of physical security correlate to Life Lines at the approximate ages shown in Figure 30. In my previous example, the man suffered the physical change of the divorce at the age of the break on his Life Line.

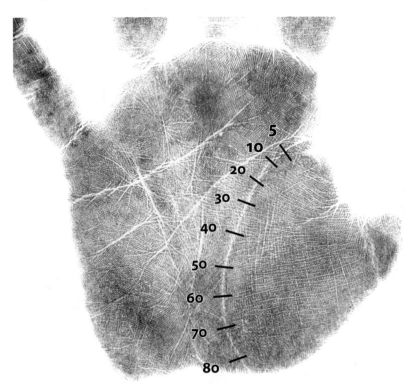

Figure 30: Time line of ages along the Life Line

Following are examples of two people who experienced significant life-changing events at the ages indicated at the breaks in the Life Lines. Figure 31 shows a root system with an earth-shattering shift in the owner's life style during the time of the break.

This significant interruption is clearly shown in the Life Line, which is composed of two separate and overlapping segments. The upper segment appears washed out by a wide white space. A secondary Life Line, on the inside, continues toward the base of the palm. At the time this print was made, the woman whose hand it is was worn out from grieving for the death of her husband of thirty-seven years. She was sixty-two when he died. She shared this:

> We started having troubles in our marriage three years before he died, but I didn't realize what was happening. He had become argumentative toward everyone, including me. I started grieving the loss of our marriage even before he died. Then he

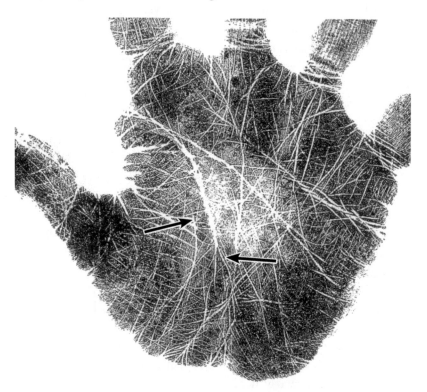

Figure 31: Broken and overlapping Life Line

was diagnosed with inoperable lung cancer. Within a week he died. I felt certain my life was over. I had been part of a unit for thirty-seven years. Now everything in my life was compromised. I was numb. I had to figure out what I liked to do and who I was. Life as I knew it was over!

The upper arrow in Figure 31 shows an inside segment of the Life Line that continues down toward the bottom of her hand. This inner line acts as a bridge, providing inner strength when needed. This told me she was quite capable of recovering from her loss. Purposeful physical routines such as walking, gardening, building something, or other Earth-related activities would help. Indeed, five years later she is well on the way to a new life. She has started over from scratch. She remodeled her entire house, starting with the kitchen, which was "his" kitchen. She recognized that she was disconnected from her body, and so continues to make a concerted effort to keep her body riveted to the earth through gardening, walking, and visiting with family. She recently said, "I'm learning to find me."

Figure 32 shows the hand of a man who told me of a life-threatening event that occurred to him when he was a child. Notice the break in his Life Line between the age of five and ten.

When I was about six years old, I was walking along the edge of Salinas River on a hot summer day with my brother, who was about eight. He knew how to swim, but I didn't. Unbeknownst to us, our two older teenage brothers, seven and eight years older, were also at the river. Before I knew it, my teenage brothers grabbed my other brother's arms and legs and heaved him into the rushing river. I started to run away, but they tackled me to the ground. In an instant, my arms and legs were clutched. They were laughing, but I was screaming for my life as they chucked me into the river. I was paralyzed with panic. As I flew through the air, my brother who was in the river yelled, "Go with the current!" I splashed into the water, tumbled around, and somehow came to the surface near the water's edge. The current swept me downstream, along with my brother. My head hit tree roots and other debris. Our survival depended on staying hidden from our terror-

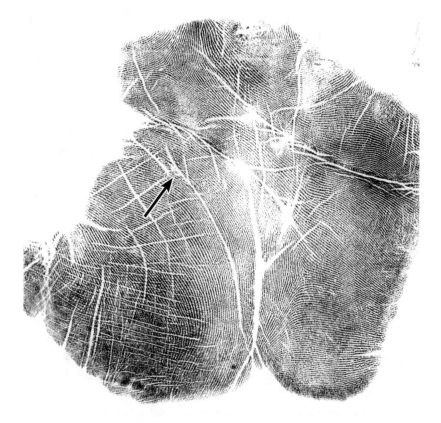

Figure 32: Screaming for his life at age six

izing teenage brothers, who were watching for us along the riverbank. We floated downstream as far as we could, until we thought it was safe to get out and hike home. I remember crying and being exhausted as I climbed out of the water onto the riverbank.

Today this man is a great swimmer. In his adult life he has played key roles in planning for and monitoring the safety of people at large events, as well as providing security for his own children. His broken Life Line reveals the reason for his continual need for safety and security.

A short or weak Life Line represents a shorter than average anchor line to the earth. When the tether to the earth is weak, there is an inclination to "hover above" the world, or to feel lost at sea. Oftentimes there was a requirement early in life to take on so much responsibility that time for play had to be sacrificed.

One client with a short Life Line told me how survival issues show up for him. He explained,

> Before I know it, I'm rationalizing starting the day earlier and earlier and ending later and later. I'm working fourteen-hour days as an average. There is a constant and never-ending continuation of tasks leading to my insanity.

When I asked what has helped him, he said,

> I've learned to see my big jobs as smaller jobs. I break large chunks of responsibility and work into smaller chunks. I can breathe easier as I settle down with bite-sized jobs.

Breaking tasks into manageable portions is a healthy strategy for addressing the overwhelming frenzy that can gradually consume a person with a short Life Line. In this spirit, my friend William Sullivan wisely said, "When looking at building many a mile of fence, it's best to take it one post at a time."

A person with a weak (short, broken, frayed, or unclear) Life Line constantly seeks stability because of a sense of being out of balance. A sense of urgency arises from the thought that there is not enough time to live fully. There is an impulse to live a high-quality life before it's too late.

This makes me think of the family comedy film *Home Alone*. An eight-year-old boy discovers that his family has left for Christmas vacation to Paris and forgotten him. Paralyzed by panic, he clasps one hand to each cheek and screams, "Ahhhh!" But after going through the terror of being left alone, he realizes he is safe, and even relishes his situation. He keeps his cool and sets booby traps for two would-be thieves who attempt to break into the house.

When the owner of a weak Life Line becomes aware of this challenge and makes a determined effort to overcome it through grounding activities, she can set her anchor and feel more stable. Examples of grounding activities include walking, yoga, working regular hours, getting enough sleep, eating healthy foods, looking out the window to watch nature in action, and simply breathing. Creating a sacred garden on the patio or painting the walls in earth colors will bring the sense of balance and harmony to a fidgety nervous system.

One is in harmony when one is consistently in sync with and closely linked to one's environment. A short or weak Life Line is a warning to focus on relaxing into the realization of sufficiency: "There is enough time," "I have enough information," "I am safe," "I am sufficient," "I am okay."

> **Key Words:** Restlessness, uprootedness, insistence, burnout
>
> **Weak Life Line Positive:** I'm on heightened alert, attentive to getting many things accomplished, with opportunities to rebuild.
>
> **Weak Life Line Negative:** I'm susceptible to burn out when I do too much (too much is defined by you, not the world); feeling out of balance and depleted.
>
> **Mantra:** With ease, I equalize work, play and rest. I breathe in the nature of life.

Family Confusion

Figure 33 shows the palm of someone who is submerged in family fluctuation. See the fractured integration of the Head and Life lines at their origination point. This woman has three adult children, all living in different cities hundreds of miles apart. She told me, "I have been challenged forever, juggling my thoughts about where to live so that I could be near one of my children. I don't want to miss out on any of my children, grandchildren, or great-grandchildren's lives." She has moved numerous times to be near each of her children. When I asked her how she decides to move, she said, "I just jump when it comes time to move." This configuration indicates fluctuation and confusion within the family because the quality of the entangled lines is scattered and ragged, and it stretches for one to one and a half inches into the palm.

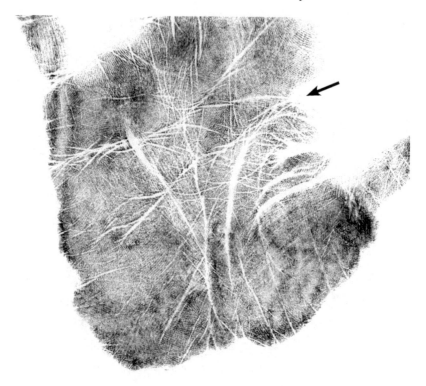

Figure 33: Family Confusion

Key Words: Unpredictibility, vacillation, changeability

Family Confusion Positive: I place high priority on my family bonds.

Family Confusion Negative: I get caught up in uncertainty and forget to enjoy my life.

Mantra: Even though I am challenged by lack of clarity about family choices, I live fully and completely where I am.

Busy, Busy Bee

The owner of a Life Line that is merged with the Fate Line is instinctively—and, some would say, excessively—responsible. The early lives of owners of this configuration were filled with family responsibilities.

As the individual grows up, he or she is destined to fulfill his or her calling by building a career portfolio, although he or she doesn't necessarily think of it that way. The journey involves serious efforts to grow and cultivate a résumé symbolizing a lot of work. This is something that this person can't ignore.

The person with this Life Line and Fate Line configuration is wired for excessive work. There is an endless list of things to do. It's likely this person had to assume adult responsibilities when they were young, as early as eight years of age, or even younger. These responsibilities may have included taking care of younger siblings, aunts, uncles, or even parents. This person's survival depended on his or her abilities to do such things as buy groceries, prepare meals, do homework, clean the house, fix a bicycle, care for a parent, and more. Such projects never cease.

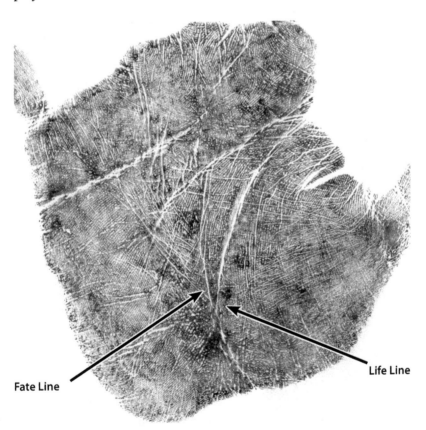

Figure 35: Busy, Busy Bee

One of my clients with this configuration told me,

I seem to be addicted to getting things done, because what would happen if I didn't? I'm pretty sure the world would fall apart. My responsibilities started very early. Mom had a nervous breakdown before I was born. In the 1950s they treated her with shock therapy. I was born ten months after her shock therapy. She told me I was such a good baby that it really helped her, and that I grew up helping her. I had an older brother who reacted to the dysfunction in the family with more dysfunction. I reacted by being the one who kept the peace. I was worried about leaving the house to spend the night with friends, because I felt my presence was needed to hold the house together. Three sisters came after me, and so the role of "eldest" fell to me. Laziness was a sin at our house. Forty years later, when Mom died, I went home from the hospital with Dad, who had Alzheimer's. I was frequently asked, "How can you hold down a job, drive your daughter to school, and take care of your dad all at the same time?" I didn't know how *not* to do that! I felt hard-wired to do it.

> **Key Words:** Determination, responsibility, exertion, overwork
>
> **Busy, Busy Positive:** I take my duties seriously and am determined to accomplish them.
>
> **Busy, Busy Negative:** My vitality is consumed by tasks. I am addicted to work.
>
> **Mantra:** I consciously create balance in the massive amount of work I do, and I schedule well-deserved time to play.

Clear Life Line

Well-rooted, long, clear, and unobstructed Life Lines belong to people who are in sync with their environments and maintain stability in their lives even in stressful situations. There is a natural rhythm to the

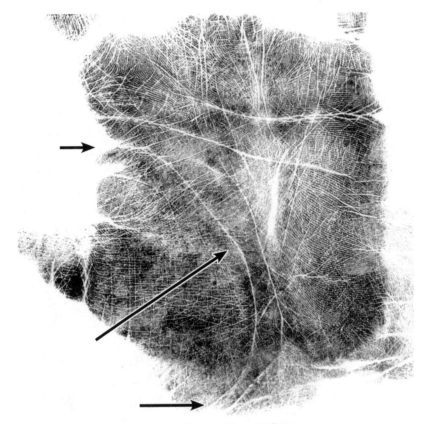

Figure 35: Long, clear Life Line

routine activities of these people's lives. They dig in, and live life to the fullest.

Figure 35 shows the palm of a woman whose awareness of the natural world is instinctive. She has spent many hours photographing nature. She is calm in both her speech and gestures, as though her feet were securely fastened to the bedrock of the earth. Her rounded Life Line indicates a robust nature and staying power.

Long Life Lines belong to people who are tuned into their bodies and effectively utilize their vitality system, such as rock climbers, marathon runners, skiers, and yoga teachers. However, you may also see athletes with short Life Lines as they apply their innate restlessness to spur their physical powers.

If your Life Line is long, deep, and clear you are strong in vitality and physical condition. You find it easy to stand firm during difficult life changes. I haven't noted a negative interpretation of the long Life Line, so I have not included one here.

Double Life Line

A person who has two Life Lines that lie side by side has extra stamina and resilience, and is always on the go. The woman whose palm is shown in Figure 36 is a seventy-four-year-old Energizer Bunny. By day she is a housekeeper, and by night she plays the washboard in a band at a local pub. Her main Life Line is joined to the Head Line for about an inch, which indicates family dependence. She is tightly bound to children, grandchildren, great-grandchildren, and many younger gal-pals who call her Mom. The secondary Life Line begins on the Mars Mount and can be considered a Line of Mars. Mars contributes to the courage of a powerful warrior.

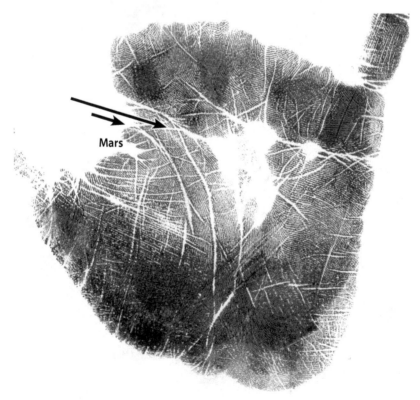

Figure 36: Double Life Line

You'll find owners of double Life Lines on the treadmill of life for the long haul. If you ask them where do they get all that energy, they just smile on the way out the door to their next activities. You wonder whether they have twins who take over while they nap. They keep going, and going, and going....

Key Words: Endurance, stamina, staying power, strength, resilience

Double Life Line Positive: It's true, I have excessive stamina and fortitude for continuous productivity.

Double Life Line Negative: When I create too much to do, for too long, I become susceptible to burn-out, which can last longer than normal.

Mantra: I use my stamina, but recognize when it's time to slow down—just a bit.

If you don't see a Life Line in your hand, don't worry. It is most likely there, but hard to see because of many neighboring lines. If your Life Line is faint, you go either way—using an abundance of energy, or conversely, feeling a lack of vigor. It is wise to conserve your energy and allow yourself adequate time to renew, based on your personal needs, after you complete a project.

Your Assignment for Deeper Discovery

1. Using the words in the book, describe some of the key words and the positive and negative interpretations of your Life Lines. *(See the example on the following page.)*

Page: _____

Right hand key words:

_____

_____

Right hand positive interpretation:

_____

_____

Right hand negative interpretation:

_____

_____

Left hand key words:

_____

_____

Left hand positive interpretation:

_____

_____

Left hand negative interpretation:

_____

_____

Example

1. Using the words in the book, describe some of the key words and the positive and negative interpretations of your Life Lines.

Page: ___87___

Right hand key words:
   <u>Broken Life Line. Life changing event, physical change</u>

Right hand positive interpretation:
   <u>Opportunity to rebuild</u>

Right hand negative interpretation:
   <u>Susceptible to burn out</u>

---

2. If what you've written in the chart describes you, transcribe it into your "My Hand Analysis Blending Guide" assignment at the back of the book, and include the mantra for your Life Line type(s).

5. The Hand Shapes

Your Elemental Profile

> "This above all: to thine own self be
> true, and it must follow, as the night
> the day, thou canst not then be false
> to any man."
>
> —William Shakespeare

BY NOW YOU are catching on to the fact that no one in the world has hands just like yours. You're seeing the various aspects of the hands and understanding the fundamental components that make up the life map etched into your hands. Now you're ready to look at the basic shape and other characteristics of your hands that reveal your persona and style of behavior. Personality and character are naturally exposed through patterns of action and preferences in relating to the world. Recognizing the meaning of your hand shape can illuminate and help you understand your personality traits and aid you in claiming positive aspects of yourself and making personal improvements, if you so desire.

Your two hands might be shaped similarly, or you might have one shape on one hand and another shape on the other hand. The shape of your right hand indicates your approach to the outer world; the shape of your left hand reveals your behavior at home or in private.

Every person's hands contain a bit of all the elements: Earth, Air, Water, and Fire. Therefore, hand shapes and characteristics rarely fit completely and perfectly into one of these four basic types, but we'll start there.

You will recognize the hand shape types more quickly with prac-

Be patient with yourself. Let your eye look for the various aspects that correspond to the basic hand shape types.

Steps for Reading Hand Shape

Step 1: Shape. Determine whether the palm is square or broad (Earth), long and rectangular like a shoebox (Air), long and narrow (Water), or rounded, pear-shaped, or irregular (Fire).

Step 2: Fingers. Relative to the length of the palm, notice whether the fingers are short and thick (Earth), long and straight (Air), long and thin like seaweed (Water), or longer than Earth but not as long as Air (Fire).

Step 3: Lines. See whether the line formations are few and deeply chiseled (Earth), many and thin (Air), many and baby fine (Water), or many and sharp (Fire).

Step 4: Skin. Check to see whether the skin is coarse with thick corrugations (Earth), smooth (Air), baby smooth (Water), or dry as though it needs lotion (Fire).

You may have noticed that steps 3 and 4 don't relate to the shape of the hand. When analyzing the hands to determine their elemental profiles and the associated personae, we also consider the lines on the palm and characteristics of the skin.

Element	Shape	Fingers	Lines	Skin
Earth	Square, broad	Short, thick	Chiseled, few	Coarse
Air	Long, shoebox	Long, straight	Thin, many	Smooth
Water	Narrow, long	Long, thin, seaweed	Tiny, fine, many	Fine and smooth
Fire	Irregular, rounded	Longer than Earth, straight	Sharp, crackling	Dry

The Primary Hand Shapes

Earth—Productive

The Earth hand has a square or broad palm. The fingers are shorter than the palm. The Earth hand has the shortest finger length of the four hand types. This hand is heavy, solid, coarse, and typically marked with very few lines. The few lines include deeply chiseled Heart, Life, and Head lines and are clear to see. Sometimes you'll also see a Fate Line running vertically up the center of the hand. The skin ridges are well defined, and the thumb is usually stiff. Both men and woman can own this hand type.

Think about the earth. Consider the ground that you stand on.

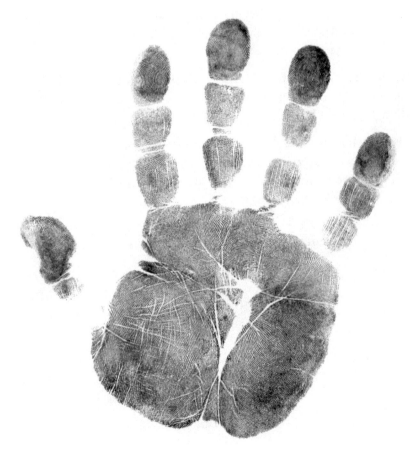

Figure 37: Earth hand shape

The earth is solid, dependable, and reliable. Jump up and you'll surely land back on the ground. The earth supports us with food and shelter. It appears motionless on the surface, but underneath its thin crust the earth is alive, with great potential for eruption. Colossal pressures keep the plates of the earth in place, but on occasion they move with tremendous fury. Beneath its surface is fertilizer for life. Because of what the earth provides, it is considered productive and protective.

You'll find people with Earth hands building things, holding tools, doing carpentry, crafting, and possibly massaging necks and shoulders. Owners of square hands like to get dirty and love to do labor such as farming, sculpting, and solving problems with hard work and exertion. They have a love of the outdoors.

If the physical landscape of your hands is square with short fingers and few deeply carved lines, you may feel as though you carry the weight of the world on your shoulders. You can easily dismiss someone who doesn't demonstrate what you consider the "right" degree of loyalty. You have a few high-quality friendships, which have taken years to develop, rather than many superficial relationships. Your thinking is practical, and expressing feelings is uncomfortable (and perhaps unnecessary). You keep things simple, are slow to change, and think in black and white and absolutes. You take pleasure in tactile contact with things like tools, products, animals, and soil.

If you live with an Earth-handed person, you'll be wise to recognize and support his or her values of privacy, honor, loyalty, security, and hard work. You might hear him or her say, "My word is my bond." Give this person space to work on projects, and allow him or her time to tinker. Your Earth mate despises the fact that when products such as dishwashers break, consumers rush out and buy new ones instead of fixing the old ones. If you break through the Earth surface with disregard for the Earth-handed person's values (listed in the Key Words below), you may see destructive energies erupt.

Key Words: Solid, practical, loyalty, simplicity, tradition, reservation, conservation

Earth Hand Positive: I am rooted in consistency, integrity, and simplicity.

Earth Hand Negative: I tend toward emotional detachment and may lack flexibility.

Mantra: With my strong sense of loyalty and common-sense nature, I open my heart to deeper levels of bonding by tapping into and communicating my feelings with those I trust.

Air—Analytical

The Air hand has a rectangular palm with straight fingers that are longer than the Earth and Fire fingers. Look for a shoebox shape of the hand and fingers. The skin is smoother than that of Earth and Fire hands. There are usually many lines in the Air palm, but they are thinner than the crackling lines of the Fire palm and not as deep.

Think of the air that flows, swirls, twirls, and spins around us every day. Air is essential for carrying information from point A to point B. The sounds of the voices of two people move on invisible airwaves. Things, ideas, sounds, scents, and people connect in and through air. What you are reading right now is seen through air. Messages on the radio and Internet talk shows move from the communicator to the masses through the medium of air. In short, air enables highly complex forms of communication such as speech, radar, and even dog whistles undetectable to the human ear. High in the sky, invisible to the eye, air can also turn into wind shear, crossing the path of aircraft en route to their destinations.

You'll most likely find people with Air hands engaged in cerebral activity. They streamline information. Politics, debates, theorizing, educating, writing, reporting, unraveling mental knots, and mediating relations between people are activities they may enjoy. They long for and must have something to analyze, understand, and communicate.

If you have an Air hand, you have a gift for observation and an eye for detail. You are keenly aware of words, sounds, body language, and subtle communication. You enjoy complex forms of communication and are quick-witted. Thinking, translating, and transmitting messages are right up your alley. As long as you cultivate an appropriate level of sensitivity, you can be an excellent mediator. When others

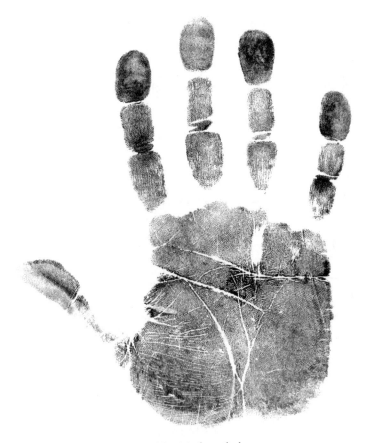

Figure 38: Air hand shape

don't appear to understand the workings of your mind, you are quickly irritated, responding with closed-mindedness, aloofness, or drama.

If you live with an Air-handed person, you'll be wise to keep an open mind, take part in debate, and not take the Air hand's occasional sarcasm personally. Realize he or she is curious and motivated by information.

The owner of the Air hand in Figure 38 and his wife, who also has an Air hand shape, constantly exchange information though both words and body language. Each fully claims his or her natural behavior style for observation and examination with quick, witty words between themselves and their friends. Between the two of them, they have lively conversation full of banter and debate. At their worst, the Air-handed person's words turn into squawks of jabbing judgments.

Key Words: Intellect, abstract, analysis, investigation, judgment, sarcasm

Air Hand Positive: I have an agile mind with the ability to examine, see and comprehend from different perspectives.

Air Hand Negative: I can be sarcastic, overly critical, and fault-finding.

Mantra: With an active mind, I am engaging life with clarity and consideration and communicating with compassion.

Water—Sensitivity

The Water hand has a long and narrow palm, with long, thin, wavy fingers that resemble seaweed. The skin is silky smooth, with many fine lines in the palm. The Water hand is often soft and flexible. The Head Line frequently curves downward toward the lower area of the palm.

Water is fluid and calm when contained. It takes the shape of its container. At the same time, water seeks to escape through evaporation, and after rising it falls back to the surface as dew or rain. Water can be deceptive with its calm surface, as strong currents and deep turbulence may swirl below. The sea is often unpredictable, and it is capable of unleashing destructive forces.

Water droplets come together to form bonds. A pool of water reflects its surroundings like a mirror. The famous martial artist Bruce Lee was often quoted as saying, "Be like the water." He taught his students to adapt and mold themselves to their opponents. When you find a Water hand, you'll see someone who can blend into her surroundings like a chameleon and conform to the needs of others. Maintaining calm seas is a primary objective of this fluid soul. You'll find Water types writing poetry, engaging in creative arts, ad-lib acting, mothering, and keeping the home peaceful.

If the narrow, long, and sensitive Water hand belongs to you, you are motivated by emotional connections, an exceptional listener, and can offer caring counsel. You quickly absorb and reflect stronger, more

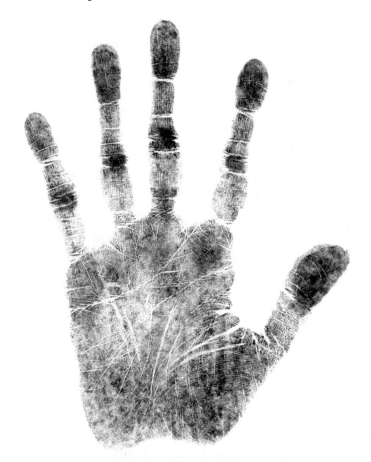

Figure 39: Water hand shape

dominant personalities, as well as those that are irritable or moody. Because external feelings and moods often distract you, paying attention to everyday details such as balancing your checkbook may not be your strong suit. You may find yourself worrying excessively that you said the "wrong" thing. You should carefully consider your boundaries, so that you don't devote yourself in filling up the many containers longing for your care. Allow yourself ample time to daydream. Follow your intuition.

If you live with someone with a Water hand with baby-fine skin, be sensitive to the emotions that stir him or her deeply. Because bonding is so important, disconnect gently. His or her mood changes according to the moods of people around him or her, so allow for his or her adaptable and changeable nature, which may vary according to all aspects of the environment, including people, places, and things.

> **Key Words:** Empathy, care, sympathy, intuition, imagination, impressionability
>
> **Water Hand Positive:** My empathetic, intuitive, and nurturing nature makes me a natural diplomat.
>
> **Water Hand Negative:** It's easy to get caught up in emotional drama and lose my own identity to those around me.
>
> **Mantra:** While it is natural to extend compassion to others, I respect my sensitivity and create boundaries to explore my own feelings.

Fire—Magnetic

The Fire hand has a rounded and longish palm, with many lines crisscrossing the palm. This shape of this hand may look irregular, like that of an apple or pear. It has shorter fingers relative to the length of the palm than the Air and Water shapes but not as short as those of the square Earth hand. The skin may look and feel dry. Many deep, sharp, energetic lines cover the palm, as if slashed with Zorro's sword. These lines display the liveliness and passion of their owner.

Consider the qualities of fire. Flames are mesmerizing. Fire excites and delights our mind, body, and soul. Fire gives and takes energy from its surroundings. People like to sit around a campfire to keep warm and have fun, but fire can be destructive when uncontrolled. Fire is active, spontaneous, untamed, attractive, and on display. Fire dies out when a lid or a wet blanket covers it.

The owner of a Fire hand likely acts on impulse and instinct. He or she may not look before leaping. The owner of the hand in Figure 40 told me, "I react, say things, and think later." The challenge of a Fire-handed person is to demonstrate exuberance in balance: neither too much nor too little, but "just right." Just right is measured by internal requirements, not by what is acceptable to the outside world.

You'll find Fire types in any field of action, expressing their cre-

Figure 40: Fire hand shape

ativity and often taking the lead. They are typically enthusiastic jacks-of-all-trades, solving problems intuitively rather than intellectually.

If Zorro has made his marks on your hands, be a catalyst for change with the zest and zeal that come naturally to you. Give yourself permission to live with passion, allowing your flame to glow. You have places to be, people to see, and things to do. Slow down enough to finish projects, and finish one at a time. Details and practicalities are probably not your thing. While delegating may come easily to you, there are some things that need your personal attention.

If you share home or office space with a Fire type, don't restrict her passion with routine or regularity. If she appears unreliable in her excitement, realize she is simply allowing her creativity to flow. She is motivated by impulse and variety. Don't ask her to conform to your expectations. If you do, you may have a wildfire to contend with. Give her radiant flames space and time to sparkle. Allow her to multitask. Her enthusiasm needs many creative outlets.

Key Words: Spontaneity, charisma, creativity, individuality, spiritedness, changeability

Fire Hand Positive: I am extremely creative; my enthusiasm keeps the momentum going, and I can be the life of the party.

Fire Hand Negative: I am challenged to focus clearly and finish tasks.

Mantra: I live fully with creative passion and a sense of joyful accomplishment when I finish what I set out to do.

Blending Hand Shapes

Now that you have explored the four basic hand shapes, you must realize that many hands do not conform to one shape. In fact, most hands blend two hand shapes. You might see long straight fingers (Air) on a square palm (Earth), or an irregular palm (Fire) with short, thick fingers (Earth), and so on. Identify the two most prominent elements, blend key points of both elements together. Note both the positive and negative interpretations of each element to better understand how a person with a blended hand shape can live with more balance.

To read for someone else, simply talk through the description, key words, positive interpretation, and negative interpretation of the hand shape you recognize. For example, "Your hand and fingers look as if they could fit into a shoebox [Air]. This tells me that it is important for you to organize thoughts and words. I also see three deeply chiseled lines in your hands [Earth]. This represents the importance you place on dependability and reliability. When I put those two elements together, you are like Radar in *MASH*. You observe, collect, organize, and analyze information [Air] as a loyal, steadfast worker, maintaining safety [Earth] for the unit." The person for whom you are reading will undoubtedly identify with your assessment as you talk through what you see.

Identifying the traits associated with your own hand shape will help you to better understand what motivates you to act and communicate as you do. If you ignore your elemental characteristics, you deny pieces of yourself, and life becomes difficult. As an example, if you have Air and Fire in your hands, you need to observe and communicate (Air) with energetic flair (Fire). If you live or work in a setting that doesn't support your essential style of behavior, you end up feeling confused and empty. Knowing about and claiming your true traits and making your preferences known to yourself and others will make a great you even better, because you'll be living your truth in your natural element.

Take a moment now to identify the primary shape of your hands on the following page. Notice which element you see most prominently. It sometimes helps to determine which element you see least, and arrive at what is most important by process of elimination.

Your Assignment for Deeper Discovery

1. Using the words in the book, describe some of the key words and
   the positive and negative interpretations of your Hand Shapes. *(See
   the example on the following page.)*

Page: _____

Right hand key words:

_____

_____

Right hand positive interpretation:

_____

_____

Right hand negative interpretation:

_____

_____

Left hand key words:

_____

_____

Left hand positive interpretation:

_____

_____

Left hand negative interpretation:

_____

_____

Example

1. Using the words in the book, describe some of the key words and the positive and negative interpretations of your Hand Shapes.

Page: __102__

Right hand key words:
  Air, analytical, reasoning, into communications

Right hand positive interpretation:
  Agile mind able to see from different perspectives

Right hand negative interpretation:
  I can be overly critical and fault-finding

---

2. If what you've written in the chart describes you, transcribe it into your "My Hand Analysis Blending Guide" assignment at the back of the book, and include the mantra for your Hand Shape(s).

6. The Fingers

Your Preference for Personal Expression

> "You do not know the road ahead of
> you: you are committing your life to
> a way."
>
> —Ralph Waldo Emerson

THE CHARACTERISTICS of each of your fingers shows an associated current of energy and how that energy manifests itself in your life. Understanding the fundamental meaning of the fingers can give you insight into traits you can use in your life and how you might best apply those traits at work, home, or in relationships.

Apart from any other characteristics of the hand, long fingers typically belong to people who are patient and have a love of detail. Short fingers indicate hastiness and reliance on instinct. People with chubby fingers indulge themselves in worldly pleasures, whereas skinny-fingered people are dreamy. Knots on the fingers at the knuckles make spaces for facts and figures to swirl around in, so large knots belong to people who are exacting and methodical. When the fingers are smooth along the sides, you'll find an intuitive person. Similarly, the length, width, depth and shape of the Colorado River provide clues as to how the force of that river flows through canyons and flatlands. When you see an upright and healthy looking finger, the force of that finger is strong and readily available for use in a person's life.

Each of the fingers is associated with a particular deity from ancient Roman mythology. The index finger is named for Jupiter; the middle finger is named for Saturn; the ring finger is named for Apollo; and the pinkie finger is named for Mercury. An easy way to remem-

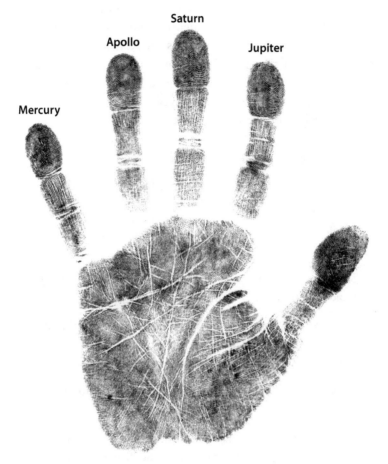

Figure 41: The fingers

ber these names is with the acronym TJSAM—T being the Thumb, which is not a finger.

To better understand the meaning of each finger, we'll consider these gods and how their attributes are associated with each finger. You have four fingers, and you carry with you the energy of all of them. However, you can determine which energy type you access most, prefer to use, and even excel at by determining which is the dominant finger on each hand, as explained in this chapter.

To begin, look at your right hand and compare the fingers to one another and identify your dominant finger. The dominant finger is the one that "looks the best." Just as you might look at four sunflowers and notice that one is most brilliant in color, stands most upright, and is at the peak of its bloom, you can also identify your best finger. The dominant finger on your right hand indicates the Roman god whose character traits you display to the world. The dominant finger on your left hand tells you which archetypal energy you access in private. It's okay if on one hand you can't decide between two fingers. Choose both and blend the energies of both as you read them.

Steps for Reading the Fingers

1. Hold your hands with the palms facing you and the fingers held high.

2. Notice which fingers stand upright, and which ones are curved or bent.

3. Identify the finger that captures your attention as the best looking. This is your dominant finger.

4. See if you have a finger that appears especially weak. Weak digits are bent, crooked, leaning to the side, bend forward, or have a section that is damaged in some way.

5. Make note of the finger(s) you see as most dominant.

Understanding the significance of the fingers is not only important for its own sake, but can also be a stepping stone to learning more about hand analysis. As you advance, you'll notice other markings below each of the fingers, and these carry messages related to the associated fingers. Sometimes you'll see vertical lines climbing up toward a finger; such lines fire up the energy of that finger. See Chapter 7 on vertical lines and how they support a vibrant energy stream connected with each finger.

For now, however, simply look for your dominant finger. If a finger stands out as weak, you are less inclined to use the associated energy, or comfortable in doing so. Learn more about this energy, and consider how you might embrace its associated qualities to support your personal expression. Understanding your risks and weaknesses can contribute to self-improvement because it allows you to address them—if you choose to do so.

The Archetypal Finger Types

Jupiter—Influence

In Palmese, your index finger is called Jupiter. Jupiter is the Roman god of the sky. There was no god greater than Jupiter, after he overthrew his father, Saturn. He had grand visions, sometimes altruistic, sometimes selfish. His goal was to have a very large territory, with many loyal followers to carry out his vision. Jupiter had lots of children, with the goal of preserving his kingdom. Central to his existence was to wield his power ambitiously in pursuit of his goals. At the slightest sign of disloyalty, Jupiter pulled lightning bolts from his backpack and boldly cast them about, thrashing everyone and everything in their path. His intent was to demonstrate his power by pulling the trigger, but his ultimate goal was to unite and lead people toward his high ideals.

Consider all the ways you use your trigger finger in a day. You can bring it to your lips to quiet children, point out directions to an inquisitive tourist, tap the "turbo" button on your hair dryer, pull the trigger on a gun, beckon to a prospective date, shake it at your sister, or aim it back toward self. There are lots of options to choose from.

Jupiterian activities include taking action on a lofty vision, activating choices to move people toward a common goal, and sitting on a throne overseeing the kingdom. You'll find Jupiterians leading teams as captains, directing people through disasters, soliciting contributions to charity, and influencing followers in worthwhile causes. It is important for someone with a strong, upright, taller-than-ring-finger index finger to be in a position of influence and power, and Jupiterian energy is a potent force for their success.

If Jupiter is your strongest finger, you're at your best when you're in a position to stimulate positive change. You create a framework into which others may step forward. Claim your power, but do so appropriately. Your actions express your ambitions and priorities. While your ideals are strong and come from a revered source, you would be well advised to learn to wield your power with consideration for others. Disrespect for your ideas, vision, and aspirations can boil your blood. On a bad day, self-centeredness and pride can get in your way and derail your plans. Develop your skill at using the abilities of your followers. If you speak out harshly, apologize and clarify your intention to implement your vision.

If you live with a Jupiterian, gain insight into his or her dreams. Consider how you can support and even promote his or her values of higher-mindedness. Like Martin Luther King, who stood for the rights of all people, you might hear your Jupiterian say, "I have a dream." Mahatma Gandhi directed us to look inside and said, "A nation's culture resides in the hearts and soul of its people." The Dalai Lama raises his index finger into the air, aiming for a better world. On the other hand, disrespected Jupiterians can become egotistical, domineering, and even dictatorial.

> **Key Words:** Ambition, leadership, vision, power, high ideals, pride, preservation, territory, expansiveness, inspiration, benevolence.
>
> **Jupiter Positive:** My vision flows effectively into action through my wholehearted, inspiring, and ambitious leadership.
>
> **Jupiter Negative:** Avoiding confrontation or overpowering others stifles my dreams.
>
> **Mantra:** My powerful visions are vibrantly expressed, with clear, well-intended, and effective direction.

Saturn—Money and Responsibility

In Palmese, your middle finger is called Saturn. In Roman mythology, Saturn is the god of time and harvest. As "old man time" he is the Great Teacher; you reap what you sow. His goal is perfection. Farmers aim for flawless crops. Business executives target the most effective use of time based on agreements and contracts. As a finger, Saturn is also considered the balance wheel. Notice how the middle finger divides the hand into two halves in Figure 42.

Have you ever seen someone give the one-finger salute? The Saturn finger has been known to rise to unsympathetic attention when one's values are disregarded. You've probably seen a driver raise her middle finger after she was cut off by another driver.

You'll find Saturnians organizing their time, applying structure to organizations, and teaching people how to be responsible with their

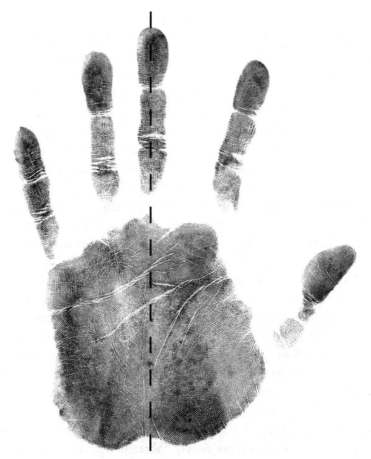

Figure 42: Saturn, the balance wheel

money, like Suze Orman. It is important for someone with a sturdy, upright, and straight Saturn finger to be in positions in which his or her skills for planning, investigation, discipline, correction, and taking care of business are efficiently utilized. Value is a key word, so you'll find Saturnians tending to important tasks at home and work. The reason money is associated with Saturn is that money flows according to values. Saturnians save money for things that have worth to them.

Saturnian activities include working to construct a better life by using time and resources efficiently; researching, clarifying and teaching people by following a system; harvesting growth after adequate time for development.

If Saturn is your dominant finger, you feel best when you are thrifty, industrious, dutiful, and following rules based on your moral code. Organizing words in an article you're writing, materials to teach, papers on your desk, shoes in your closet, or food in your pantry, are all right up your methodical alley. On a bad day, when you're feeling out of balance, you can isolate yourself to process guilt, melancholia, bitterness, or fear. Others may accuse you of being pessimistic, cynical, or doubting of yourself. Keep things in perspective, and avoid letting the seriousness of Saturn keep you down for too long. To climb out of the abyss, get a note pad and a pen and jot down what you appreciate about yourself, such as your ability to categorize, coordinate, and discriminate. Include a few things you appreciate about others, too.

If you live with a Saturnian, give her time to seriously discriminate, contemplate, and organize. Like Benjamin Franklin, who said, "A penny saved is a penny earned," she can offer a frugal game plan to the household. You might hear your Saturnian say, "All good things come to those who wait," emphasizing the benefit of patience. Suze Orman promotes her "safety box," to keep your valuables protected from fire, flood, and earthquake. Osho, a spiritual teacher, taught a system of disciplined meditation in pursuit of higher wisdom. Brea Hodges on "Desperate Housewives" wouldn't leave the house unless her dress, makeup, and hair were just right—as well as her silverware drawer being perfectly arranged. Rushing the Saturnian will only cause her to dig in her heels even more deeply. Water her garden and you will witness her wisdom.

> **Key Words:** Responsibility, accountability, structure, value, organization, discipline, patience, wisdom, teaching, money, morals, security, integrity
>
> **Saturn Positive:** Through diligence, my wisdom increases with time, contemplation, patience, and structure.
>
> **Saturn Downside:** My overly serious nature, pessimism, and fear about security can get me down.
>
> **Mantra:** My foundation is strong. I am appropriately responsible for what is important and, as needed, I bring concerns to the table with a level head.

Apollo—Individuality

In Palmese, the ring finger is called Apollo. In Greek mythology, Apollo was the favored son of Zeus. He received appreciation, approval, and applause from his parents, and was forever concerned with appearance. He was the shining performer, expressing his optimistic, brilliant, fun-loving, and colorful nature. He was in the public eye as an artist and archer. As a master archer, he focused his aim on targets by developing his skills through patience and persistence.

You'll find Apollonians performing in the spotlight, perhaps dancing, singing, speaking, or writing for an audience—but they must first overcome the fear of tomatoes. They thrive on a platform, expressing their most individualistic natures. Reputation and acknowledgment motivate their performances. So that he could be seen, the infant Apollo loved to be elevated in his mother's backpack. The teen Apollonian loves being rewarded with approval and acceptance from parental figures and peers alike. Vanity, in the right amount, is a key ingredient for creating Apollo's best self.

Apollonian activities include being true to and extending your inner muse; uniquely expressing your ultimate craft in the spotlight; schmoozing and networking. If you identify with Apollo and know you are called to claim the spotlight, persist!

Identify your craft. Make it a priority. Identify impediments. If you are hiding, find ways to come out. Address your fear of a king-sized stage hook embarrassingly dragging you off stage. Reframe your fear of flying tomatoes into an opportunity to catch nutritious food. Don't let a fear of critics derail your compelling call to unique expression. There is a just-right audience who will rave for the creation you let flow through you. Vow that your mind, body, and soul will shine bright. Your magnetic flair is attractive. Integrate a passionate plan with discipline, and put yourself out there.

If you live with an Apollonian, support her craft by running lines for her upcoming play, admiring her fashion designs, or encouraging her to splash her unique design on her canvas of choice. But know that she can become self-conscious and paralyzed by a fear of rejection.

Examples of living Apollonians claiming the spotlight are Madonna, Lady Gaga, Mick Jagger, and George Michael. Deceased Apollonians include Marilyn Monroe, who lived in a number of foster homes as a child, and Ludwig van Beethoven, who was abused by his alcoholic father. These luminaries honored the call of the source of their individuality despite the adversity in their lives. The sun can only shine when the artist is true to his or her distinctive essence.

Key Words: Individuality, creativity, originality, charisma, brilliance, vitality, spontaneity, vanity.

Apollo Positive: My fun-loving, risk-taking, magnetic individuality puts me joyfully in the spotlight.

Apollo Negative: Reputation fears, self-consciousness, and acts of conformity send me into hiding.

Mantra: I take suitable risks to display the substance of my true individualistic expression in the name of my essential creative calling.

Mercury—Communication

In Palmese, the pinkie finger is called Mercury. In Roman mythology, Mercury is known as the messenger god. He has wings on his cap and on his sandals so that he can quickly transmit messages between mind and body. Mercury is a trader of information, products, and people. He is analytical, brilliant, and eloquent, learning faster than the speed of light. He is known to be precise, quick-witted, and detached. He is swift in movement and agile in mind. He frequently traveled between the sky, the earth, and the underworld. Mercury governs commerce and trading, public media, and the worlds of diplomacy and persuasion. You'll find Mercury involved with anything related to the transmission of information.

You'll find Mercurians cleverly linking their thoughts to words in an instant. Mercurian qualities belong to brilliant comedians such as Lucille Ball and Jim Carrey, and to witty news reporter Jon Stewart, clever detective Sherlock Holmes, or super-brain Albert Einstein. They thrive on having information to communicate, unless their wings are clipped and they're restricted in some way. On a bad day a Mercurian can withhold information, distort information through trickery, or become verbose. If pinned to a regimented system, a Mercurian can become unstable, impulsive, indecisive, and overly critical.

If Mercury is your best finger, you'll tip your teacup, with your pinkie in the air eloquently pronouncing, "Please, tell me something I don't already know." As you're reading this, you're most likely ready to jump to your next adventure. Before you do, consider how your quick, sharp, clever language affects others positively and negatively. Are others able to keep up, or do you leave them in a cloud of bewilderment? Can you capitalize on your gift for communication and adapt to their level of awareness? Of course you can! You have instant access to words and the awareness that goes along with it. Watch to see when you withdraw in the face of emotional misunderstanding. You feel closest to your mate, children, and co-workers when you're free to discuss, banter, and joke. Use your expertise for rhetoric, whether in writing, editing, speaking, singing, sign language, negotiating deals, trading, or any linguistic activity.

If you live with a Mercurian, don't take either his everlasting thirst for curiosity or his verbal retreats personally. Give him room for critical thinking, analysis, and word-juggling. He needs space to negotiate and strategize. Remember, he can be quite humorous and full of wit in his own unique way. A Mercurian is constantly scheming how to manipulate language, thoughts, and ideas. At his best he is skilled at knowing how to listen and speak appropriately for the environment he's in.

Key Words: Quickness, agility, cleverness, sharpness, reflectivity, insightfulness, wit

Mercury Positive: With quick intellect I bridge a variety of ideas, thoughts, words, and activities.

Mercury Negative: Trickery and craftiness with little white lies may seem like the best strategy but are not always the wisest.

Mantra: I use my inherent communication skills and insights to listen, understand, and be heard.

Your Assignment for Deeper Discovery

1. Using the words in the book, describe some of the key words and
   the positive and negative interpretations of your dominant fingers.
   (*See the example on the following page.*)

Page: _____

Right hand key words:

_____

_____

Right hand positive interpretation:

_____

_____

Right hand negative interpretation:

_____

_____

Left hand key words:

_____

_____

Left hand positive interpretation:

_____

_____

Left hand negative interpretation:

_____

_____

Example

1. Using the words in the book, describe some of the key words and the positive and negative interpretations of your dominant fingers.

Page: <u>113–114</u>

Right hand key words:

<u>Index finger, Jupiter, visionary, influencer</u>

Right hand positive interpretation:

<u>My vision flows effectively into action through my whole-</u>
<u>hearted, inspiring, and ambitious leadership</u>

Right hand negative interpretation:

<u>Avoiding confrontation or overpowering others stifles</u>
<u>my dream</u>

2. If what you've written in the chart describes you, transcribe it into your "My Hand Analysis Blending Guide" assignment at the back of the book, and include the mantra for your dominant finger(s).

7. The Vertical Lines

Your Impulse to Flow on Purpose

> "Nothing is impossible that is wholly
> desired."
>
> —A Course in Miracles

THE VERTICAL LINES of the hands reveal an urge for expression of life force related to the fingers under which they lie. Each of the four lines is named according to the finger toward which it rises: Jupiter (index), Saturn (middle), Apollo (ring), and Mercury (pinkie). The lines may be short or long. There may be two or more lines beneath a single finger, or there may be none at all.

A vertical line represents the flow of sustenance and supporting strength, with the characteristics of the finger it supports, like the root of a plant. For example, a Jupiter Line extends the force of the Jupiter finger in the form of inspiration. The Saturn Line shows the owner's yearning for effort and responsibility. The Apollo Line spotlights the creative urge, and the Mercury Line depicts the curiosity of a seeker.

When analyzing vertical lines, consider the length, quality, and quantity. Clear, deep, and long lines carry more force than short faint lines. If there are multiple vertical lines under one finger, each carries extra force of that kind. Having extra lines isn't always better; rather, it indicates more opportunity for expression of that type of energy.

Think of these lines as electrical wiring, allowing currents of energy to flow and support the attributes of the associated fingers. The longer the vertical lines, the more energy they carry. The presence of several parallel vertical lines indicates extra energy, which may manifest as a burden of too many choices related to the particular line. The

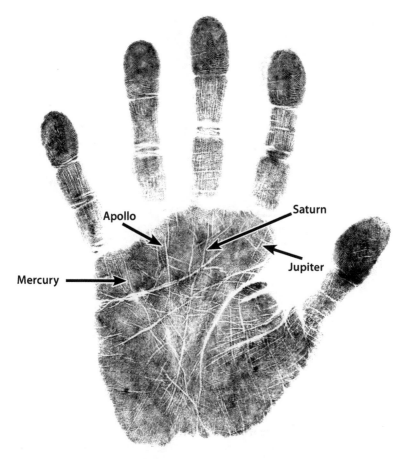

Figure 43: Vertical lines of the palm

condition of the finger itself is also significant here. The stronger and straighter the finger above the vertical line, the better and more positively the associated characteristics will be expressed. At least, there is a potential for greater expression.

Vertical Line Identification

The Jupiter Line—Inspiration

The Jupiter Line runs upward on the Jupiter Mount toward the index finger. In Roman mythology, Jupiter is known as a visionary, with high ideals for his kingdom. There's not much room for a vertical line

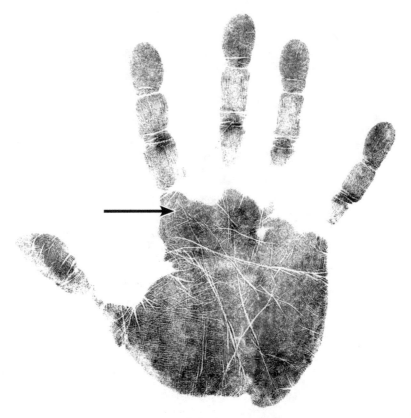

Figure 44: The Jupiter Line

on the Jupiter Mount, so even if this line is short, its owner will feel compelled to move forward, motivated by his or her vision. This line can sprout from the Life Line (as in Figure 44), or it can stand alone, either singly or in multiple lines. If you have this line in your hand, you'll do well to clarify your ideas and use your zeal and ambition to inspire others to follow their dreams. Consider expressing your innate power in an influential role such as a high profile career, or as a homemaker guiding your family and its tasks toward specific goals. You might say, "I have the need to achieve," or "You can do it!"

People whose hands contain Jupiter Lines inspire others toward their highest potentials. They are natural coaches. It's often easier to boost others to their aspirations than for them to do so themselves; but, that in itself brings fulfillment to the inspirer. Some palmistry books call this the line of ambition, but I do not. There is definitely a correlation between ambition and inspiration, as they both stem from desire. People with ambition motivate themselves and others toward a goal with determination. But I've seen many ambitious, strong-minded, driven people who lack this line, which means one doesn't have to have this line in order to be ambitious. If I were to link ambition with this line, I'd say, "It looks like you have strong ambition, based on your vision and ideals, to inspire others."

Notice that Figure 44 shows both a long vertical line under the Jupiter (index) finger and a dominant Jupiter finger. (A finger is dominant because it 'looks better' than the other three digits.) The combination of both vertical line and dominant finger denotes a confident force of Jupiter—seeing the big picture, influencing others for the good of all.

The owner of the handprint in Figure 44 is a way-shower and constantly encourages others to live their best lives. She explains, "I have worked very hard to release any attachment to others' choices. If the receiver isn't ready, I understand that my encouragement or sharing is not meant for this particular person to hear or act upon at this time."

> **Key Words:** Inspiration, vision, persuasiveness, spirituality, idealism
>
> **Jupiter Line Positive:** I offer inspiration for growth, for the highest good of all.
>
> **Jupiter Line Negative:** I am discouraged when others don't rise to their potential.
>
> **Mantra:** I encourage better lives, but allow others the dignity of making their own choices for personal growth.

The Saturn Line—Effort

The vertical line rising to the middle finger has been called the Fate Line, the Career Line, the Money Line, and more. Saturn energy urges one to accomplish tasks through extended effort and responsibility. The length, quality, and quantity of lines under this finger are interpreted to understand how the owner demonstrates responsibility

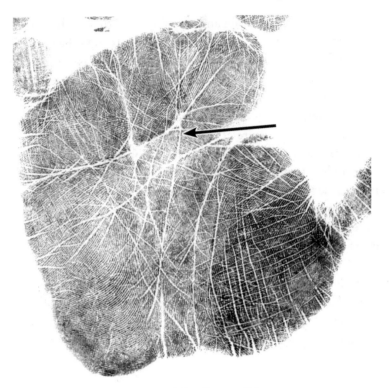

Figure 45: The Saturn Line

through effort. Effort is made through organization, structure, and discipline. Experience and knowledge support organizational skills. We typically see these Saturnian characteristics in work, projects, and careers. As effort is put forth in work, money typically appears.

In Figure 45, a long, straight vertical line starts at the base of the palm and rises all the way to the top of the palm, ending under the middle finger. This indicates an organized person, with systems in place to complete tasks with perfect outcomes. On the positive side, this person fulfills commitments and is driven by a thirst for knowledge. On the negative side, this person may take on too much responsibility or feel overly responsible for the well-being of others.

In Figure 46 several vertical lines climb toward the Saturn finger. Multiple vertical lines indicate determination and a tendency to take on multiple projects. The good news is that this person has plenty of drive. The bad news is that this person may have too many projects going on at the same time, with none getting finished, resulting in a feeling of inadequacy. The owner of multiple Saturn Lines is chal-

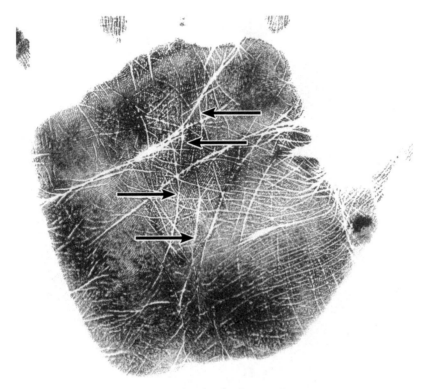

Figure 46: Multiple Saturn Lines

lenged to commit to one project and follow it through to completion. If you have multiple vertical lines climbing toward your middle finger and are divided between many endeavors, but you truly feel good about it, then be happy with that. Replace feelings of guilt and inadequacy with confidence and joy in your effort.

Notice the arrow pointing to the Saturn Line in Figure 47. The line is faint and hard to see, but in relation to the few other lines in this hand, it has potency. This young person has demonstrated dedication through discipline, structure, and organization in pursuit of a Ph.D. in neuroscience. Also notice that the middle finger, which the line is aiming for, stands upright in its natural position. A straight finger above a vertical line implies added strength of responsibility and structure.

If a hand doesn't have a vertical line rising to the Saturn finger, its owner is more inclined to drift along, without a plan. This doesn't mean she won't work hard, but if she does, it will most likely be in a direction that someone else has defined. The good news is that this person has the freedom to shape her own way in the world, at her own pace.

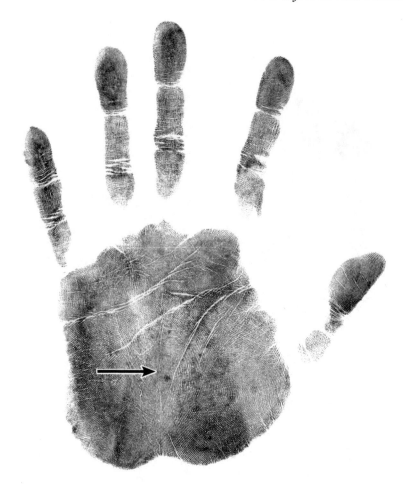

Figure 47: Faint Saturn Line

There are many possibilities for Saturn Line configurations. One key to interpreting this line is where the line ends. For example, if the line stops at the Heart Line, its owner may quit a project for the sake of love; responsibilities are rearranged for love. One of my clients whose Saturn Line stopped at the Heart Line met her husband at work.

> **Key Words:** Effort, direction, work, career, security, organization, responsibility, knowledge

> **Saturn Line Positive:** I am effectively aligned with the task, feeling secure.

Saturn Line Negative: I am dedicated to responsibilities at the expense of relationships.

Mantra: I live with joy, as I am balanced in my responsibilities.

The Apollo Line—Expression

The Apollo Line is a vertical line rising to the ring finger. It appears just below the finger. The average length is about one-half inch, but sometimes this line can extend all the way from the bottom to the top of the palm. The longer and deeper the line is, the more talent to express creative energy it shows. Apollo's job was to be true to his muse, regardless of the audience. He had tremendous inner strength and was bright and brilliant in his self-expression. He was an individualist extraordinaire. At his best he was socially integrated. A strong, deep Apollo Line shows a call to perform in one's true expression. The call is intensified when the Apollo finger is straight and upright.

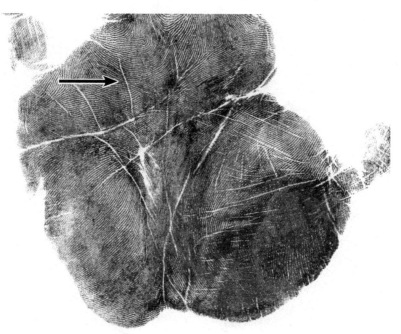

Figure 48: The Apollo Line

Figure 49: A long Apollo Line—exceptionally talented

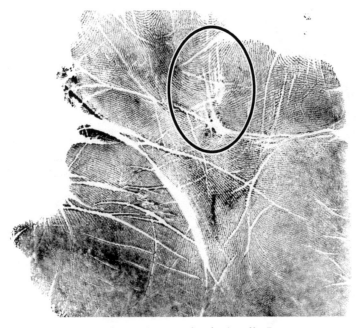

Figure 50: Multiple Apollo Lines

A person with a long Apollo Line (Figure 49) is happiest when he or she allows the inner artist to shine forth in full force. Notice how this Apollo line stands out: there are not many other lines in the hands to compete with it. This talented person is capable of being a scriptwriter, actor, makeup artist, director, and producer—all in one.

Apollo Lines, as in Figure 50, indicate that a person has many creative outlets to choose from, and the owner of such lines is hard put to choose among them. One woman I read for had five parallel vertical lines on her Apollo Mount. She couldn't decide which craft to pursue, so she opened an artisan co-op to display and sell paintings, pottery, bracelets, scarves, soap, masks, and more, for many local artists.

The owner of an Apollo Line that climbs toward the ring finger then turns toward the pinkie is at her best when creating messages with words. Figure 51 shows two Apollo lines, one climbing toward

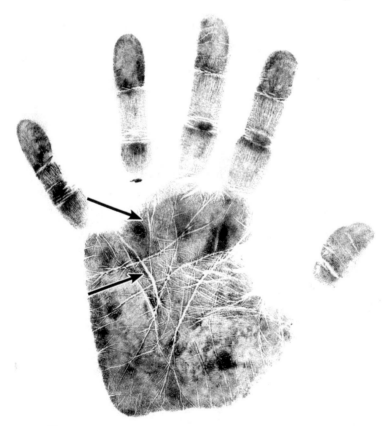

Figure 51: Apollo Lines, one bent toward Mercury

the ring finger and one curving toward the pinkie. Both originate under the ring finger. The more noticeable line aims toward the pinkie. This signifies ability and talent in communication. Remember, Mercury is the Messenger. This person's Apollo finger is the strongest of the four fingers because it's standing upright.

I've seen many artistically active people who have no Apollo Line. If you want to pursue a life in the arts but you don't have this line on your hand, don't be discouraged. You may have other indicators in your hands that support your passion to create. Follow your dream.

Key Words: Creativity, expression, performance, talent, inner strength, optimism, individuality

Apollo Line Positive: I am open and willing to be true to my inner artist.

Apollo Line Negative: I can hide in paralyzing fear of rejection.

Mantra: Optimistically, I shine in my right light.

The Mercury Line—The Seeker

The Mercury Line is a straight or curved vertical line aiming for the pinkie (Mercury) finger. You'll find Mercury Lines on people who seek information, want to understand the meaning of things, and have keen insights. It's common to find this line on people who read self-improvement books and have hand readings. As the messenger god, Mercury translates information between the spirit world and the material world; hence this vertical line and the pinkie finger represent the use of communication in both the external and internal worlds.

In Figure 52, three arrows point to a long, straight, and fairly clear Mercury Line. This shows curiosity and exceptional ability to perceive what's happening both above and below the surface of common communication.

I haven't come across a negative interpretation of the long, straight Mercury Line. This line depicts one who is insightful, curious, and a seeker of meaning.

A Mercury Line that arcs around the lower, outer edge of the

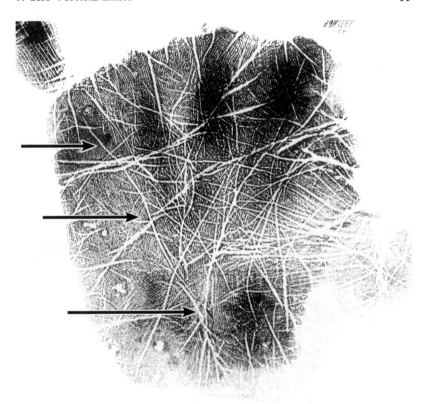

Figure 52: The Mercury Line

palm, known as the Moon or Luna Mount, shows the gift of profound insight. (See Figure 53.) People with Mercury Lines that curve like this are highly intuitive. They have exceptional talent to attune to and understand messages about the meaning of life. At their best, they claim this ability and use the gift of constant contact with "That Which Knows" as a spiritual coach or guide. At their worst, they doubt their abilities and become alienated from themselves and their core identities. (The core identity is the deepest part of the Self, and awareness of that Self.) It's not uncommon for people with this curving line to experience crises of meaning, because they have a deep longing to know the answers to life's big questions, such as "Why am I here?", "Why are we here?", and "What is my purpose?" At some point, the material world comes into view as an illusion and the real, inner world appears. When this happens, it is a sign the "meanings expert" has been activated.

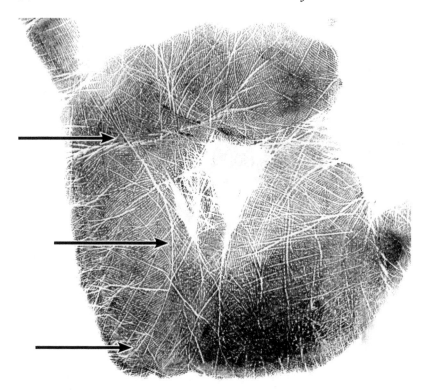

Figure 53: Curved Mercury Line

The best attributes of a Mercury Line come through when the Mercury finger is straight. If the pinkie finger is bowed, twisted, or damaged, then the current running through the line will be impeded, making it more difficult to access inner awareness. The pinkie finger can straighten up with time, but this requires determination for honest, conscious, communications on a continuous basis, with others and with one's self.

> **Mercury Line Key Words:** Curiosity, insight, intuition, communications, meaning
>
> **Curved Mercury Line Key Words:** Exceptional awareness, heightened intuition, profound understanding, alienation
>
> **Curved Mercury Line Positive:** I am acutely tuned in to higher messages and responding appropriately.

Curved Mercury Line Negative: In disillusionment I isolate myself by hanging out with deadbeats.

Mantra: I listen, hear, trust, and follow my inner guidance all the time.

Your Assignment for Deeper Discovery

1. Using the words in the book, describe some of the key words and
   the positive and negative interpretations of your vertical lines. *(See
   the example on the following page.)* If the vertical lines are hard to see,
   use a magnifying glass or make handprints (see the instructions in
   Chapter 1), or simply skip this assignment.

Page: _____

Right hand key words:

_____

_____

Right hand positive interpretation:

_____

_____

Right hand negative interpretation:

_____

_____

Left hand key words:

_____

_____

Left hand positive interpretation:

_____

_____

Left hand negative interpretation:

_____

_____

Example

1. Using the words in the book, describe some of the key words and the positive and negative interpretations of your vertical lines.

Page: __129-132__

Right hand key words:
  __Apollo   urge for creative expression__

Right hand positive interpretation:
  __I am open and willing to be true to my inner artist__

Right hand negative interpretation:
  __I can hide in paralyzing fear of rejection__

2. If what you've written in the chart describes you, transcribe it into your "My Hand Analysis Blending Guide" assignment at the back of the book, and include the mantra for your vertical line(s).

8. Reading Hands Mindfully

The Next Step

> "I thank god for my handicaps for,
> through them, I have found myself,
> my work, and my God."
> —Helen Keller

NOW THAT YOU have explored your hands in some detail you may want to take what you have learned to the next level. Whether you're new to hand analysis or already a professional, you need to cultivate the right approach to reading hands.

Clarify your intentions. Why are you interested in learning to read hands? Do you want to learn for fun? Maybe you've decided to become a professional hand analyst. Are you compelled to help others understand themselves more deeply? You may be a seeker of meaning. Or perhaps you are a skeptic exploring this subject with a rational and reasoning mind. Some people have told me that they just *had* to learn. They felt "drawn" to the subject naturally, like a rose turns toward the sun. Others have simply been curious, and wanted to feed their curiosity. Understanding your intentions will steer you in the right direction. What you intend is attracted into your life.

Plan to practice. Set aside time on your calendar to read hands, contemplate, and integrate your new insights. You will integrate your intellect and intuition when learning and delivering a reading. Both logic and insight contribute greatly to learning and applying your new skill. Attention and practice will help you succeed. Confucius said, "I see and I forget. I hear and I remember. I do and I understand."

Refer to this book. Use this book to learn on your own, with a friend, or with a group. Refer to this material often as you look into the hands that are opened to you. Use it to impart your newfound knowledge. Collect feedback from the people you read for, and make notes for future reference. This book is your reference manual. Professionals use instruction manuals regularly. Their careers and right lives depend on the appropriate use of their technical guidebooks.

Launch an expedition. Consider yourself going on a journey. In a sense, I have been your guide, escorting you around the landscape of hands. This is new territory. Be prepared to learn some very interesting things about yourself and others. The more willing you are to look within yourself, traveling to your core, the better you will be able to guide others to do the same thing—and feel safe along the way. You'll see amazing expressions on people's faces as you disclose secrets about them based on the etchings in their palms. Honor what you discover about someone, and keep it secret, because it's not for anyone else to know. You might see grimaces on people who say, "That is so *not* me!" Well, it might not appear that way to them. However, all of us have a shadow side; something we're hiding that our subconscious mind isn't prepared to disclose. Don't be surprised if the owner of that grimace returns to you and says, "I thought more about what you read in my hands, and you *were* right."

Be present. You'll read the likes, dislikes, talents, strengths, weaknesses, and conflicts in children, teens, and adults. You'll get into someone else's brain and understand how they express themselves. An Earth-handed person is private and may be taken aback when you see them so unmistakably; just relax and stay with them. An Air-handed person will want to analyze and understand, so she'll likely have many questions for you. A Water-handed person may shed a few tears, so you'll want to have tissues available. You're learning how to speak in someone else's language. Adapting to someone else's inner language allows you to see them. What can be more loving than being present with a person and seeing who he or she really is?

Be humble. You'll enhance your journey into new realms as you let go of your own self-importance. New dimensions will be added to your existence. People may divulge secrets to you because you "see" them. You'll be awestruck by the truth. In short, you'll discover a new world. Foster a humble presence.

Be compassionate. Effectively describing the markings on someone's hands will require you to let go of your judgments. You might believe that taking care of others is important and should be a high priority. But a person who takes care of others at the expense of herself could be annihilating her own soul and locking herself into an unsatisfying life. Or you could see a passionately longwinded person as obnoxious, failing to understand that their type of enthusiasm is crucial for their overall well-being. You may see a marking indicating how a person's desire system is impressed so deeply by others that they have lost sight of their own wishes. Bring compassion to your readings.

Set boundaries. When others learn of your new skill as a hand reader, you will find a lot of hands reaching for your attention. Read as you are called to read. It's up to you to decide when the time is right to read hands. Take *your* time. Tune in to your inner self, and share your new talent as you are guided from within.

Articulate your message. Once you've completed your "My Hand Analysis Blending Guide" don't be shy about speaking out about what you've learned about yourself. Share your insights with others. As you excel and advance in the world of hand analysis, you'll see opposites, conflicts, and contradictions in people. This is the most important part of hand analysis, because you'll be able to describe clearly people's internal dilemmas. Your words may save a person's life. How you express your insights is crucial to your delivery. Your client could be clinging to every word you say. The point here is to be sensitive to how your client receives the information you are seeing and discussing.

Visualize yourself. See yourself as an outstanding hand analyst. Hold the idea that you are really good at this. Consider having your own hands read by professionally trained and certified hand analysts so that you can observe their methods. You'll develop your own style over time. Imagine yourself as a hand reader in the way you want to be recognized.

Be curious. The best way to learn is to be open to new possibilities. Inquire into the hand. Be a sacred vessel of profound insights. Keep your mind, body, and soul prepared for the best that can happen. But, know that you might hear negative responses too. Be curious about what those reactions mean. There is no need to take negative comments personally. Be curious as you hold tight to your original intention.

Ease. Enter into this practice with grace and determination. Take time to apply it; discover for yourself and formulate your own conclusions. As you read other people's hands, you'll be presenting yourself as a guide for inner and outer transformation. Seeing someone move beyond a painful heartbreak, job loss, communication breakdown with a child, or confusion of any kind because of something you read in his or her hands might be some of the most rewarding work you do.

Enjoy. Foster an internal flame of delight. Bring your inner smile to all you meet.

9. How to Host a Hand-Reading Circle Using This Book

Inspire Purposeful Living

> *"Be really whole and all things will come to you."*
>
> —*Lao-Tzu*

FOLLOWING ARE GUIDELINES for hosting a hand-reading circle with your friends or colleagues. Everyone will learn something new about him- or herself and about the others. Interpersonal bonds will deepen. This could be one of the most memorable occasions you and your friends have ever shared. Consider hosting a reading circle for a bridal shower, birthday party, or Valentine's Day celebration, or for an anniversary, graduation, retirement, or holiday party.

To invite people to your hand-reading circle, follow the steps below.

Select seven to ten friends, clients, or workmates to invite. Let them know about *Your Life is in Your Hands* and the highlights of what you have learned about yourself from the book. Invite your guests to purchase this book at www.YourLifeIsInYourHands Book.com, or give the book to them as a gift, so they can prepare for the event.

Set the date and time for your hand-reading circle. Allow fifteen to twenty minutes per person, plus forty minutes for mingling and enjoying appetizers (provided by you, or pot luck).

Send invitations, ask your guests to RSVP, and ask everyone to finish reading the book and doing the assignments a few days before the gathering. The following is an example to consider for your invitation:

Dear Friend,

You're invited to a sacred hand-reading circle.

DATE: [Day of the week and date]

TIME: Starting promptly at [time] lasting about [number]
hours

WHAT TO BRING: Yourself, your completed assignments from
Your Life Is In Your Hands by Kay Packard, and a yummy
dish to share. You will be invited to talk about what you
learned about yourself with the group in a private and
sacred setting. This will be an incredible way for us to
support and nurture each other and ourselves on our life
journey.

Send a reminder to everyone who plans to attend via e-mail or text-message, letting them know how much you are looking forward to seeing them at the hand-reading circle on the date you selected.

On the day of your hand-reading circle, follow these steps to set up and run the event.

Prepare the space for your circle. You may want to arrange your living room furniture into a circle, have pillows or folded blankets on the floor to sit on, or use your dining room or boardroom table to congregate. A circular configuration is best because everyone will feel equal.

Set the stage for a supportive, uplifting, and safe experience. Have tissue boxes available incase anyone sheds a tear or two. You may want to have food out on a separate table so that people see it when they arrive.

Within five or ten minutes of your planned start time, invite everyone to come into the circle and take a seat. Talk through the format in which your guests will share their insights. You might include the following:

Thank you for coming together today to share a bit of yourself with our friends and me. It is truly an honor to host this event with you, my very special friends [and/or clients or colleagues]. I wanted to host this circle because
_____. I hope you find this to be an insightful experience, and that you leave feeling uplifted, more

empowered, and inspired to live purposefully. Each of you has now read through *Your Life Is In Your Hands* and completed the assignments at the back of the book. Each of you will be invited to share what you learned as a result of completing the assignments. It is important for all of us to agree that we will not share what we hear today with anyone outside this circle. This is a sacred setting in which we can allow ourselves to open our hearts and be truly seen.

Each person will have fifteen minutes to share, plus an additional five minutes for supportive feedback from the others in the circle. This will be each person's turn to tell about their new awarenesses, so let us allow them to share his or her thoughts and insights without interruption. I will set a timer so that everyone has an equal amount of time to share. When we have heard from half of the group, we'll take a thirty- to forty-minute break to mingle and enjoy the food. Does anyone have any questions? Would anyone like to volunteer to go first? Otherwise, I'll share first. Okay, let's begin.

After the circle send a card, e-mail, or text-message, to each of your guests thanking them for being open and willing to share. You may also want to remind them of the sacredness of what was revealed, and remind them to keep it a secret.

Appendix

Assignments to Ignite your Inner Wisdom

> *"…just as the artist must first master the art of*
> *blending his colours, so must the practitioner*
> *master the art of blending words. They are the tools*
> *of our trade and the medicine of our profession"*
> —Noel Jaquin, (1893–1974)
> *famous hand analyst*

THE ASSIGNMENTS for this book are intended to help you activate your inner wisdom. Completing some or all of these assignments will help you blend together the interpretations of the markings you identified in your hands. After you understand and accept natural aspects of yourself, you can live your life with less effort and more meaning.

To complete these assignments most effectively, you may want to set aside some time to dig into them. But if you're short on time, you can simply jot down quick notes and look for threads pointing to an empowering life theme for you. As you fill in the assignments, I encourage you to use the exact words, verbatim, of the descriptions with each marking given in this book. But there is no wrong way to do it. The assignments are designed to guide you step by step to your authentic interior self.

It's also a good idea to take notes as you read through the book, in a journal, on a computer, or on a blank piece of paper, and jot down key words about what you're seeing in your hands.

Following are instructions and samples of filled-in assignment sheets. For printable copies of blank forms, visit http://YourLifeIs InYourHandsBook.com/free-assignment-sheets.

Assignment 1
My Hand Analysis Blending Guide

TO BLEND THREE of the most prominent markings you see in your hands, refer to the fill-in charts at the end of each chapter, or your journal or notes, and pick configurations in your hands that just pop out at you. After you complete the exercise with three, you may want to add two or three more. You may choose different markings three or six months from now. For now, allow yourself to start with three. See the example on the following pages before you create your own.

My Hand Analysis Blending Guide (example)

1. Name of marking #1 I see in my hands:
   Big Heart Heart Line

   Description of marking #1:
   Caring, nurturing, and connecting

   Positive Interpretation
   I help people feel loved and cared for while
   spending some time alone nurturing myself

   Negative interpretation:
   I can easily lose myself in the drama of others
   and feel like a victim

   My mantra:
   I claim my boundaries, realizing I am the love
   I seek and long to embody

2. Name of marking #2 I see in my hands:
   Air Hand Shape

   Description of marking #2:
   Analytical, curious, quick witted, investigative

   Positive interpretation:
   I have an agile mind with the ability to examine,
   see, and comprehend from different perspectives

   Negative interpretation:
   I can be sarcastic, overly critical, and fault-finding

   My mantra:
   With an active mind, I am engaging life with
   clarity and consideration and communicating
   with compassion.

Blend markings #1 and #2:
   Big Hearted and nurturing communicator
   offering loving counsel

My Hand Analysis Blending Guide (example, cont.)

3. **Name of marking #3 I see in my hands:**
   Long, clear Head Line, Super Synthesizer

   Description of marking #3:
   Multifaceted system of comprehension and
   analysis

   Positive interpretation:
   Exceptional skill for synthesizing information

   Negative interpretation
   I create problems to solve in relationships

   My mantra:
   I exercise my ability to engage in the complex
   synthesis of thoughts without creating tangled
   webs within my closest relationships.

   Blend markings #1, #2, and #3:
   Big hearted (Big Heart), considerate (Air Hand
   Shape) master problem solver (Super Synthesizer).

My Hand Analysis Blending Guide

1. Name of marking #1 I see in my hands:

_____

Description of marking #1:

_____

Positive Interpretation

_____

_____

Negative interpretation:

_____

_____

My mantra:

_____

_____

2. Name of marking #2 I see in my hands:

_____

Description of marking #2:

_____

Positive interpretation:

_____

_____

Negative interpretation:

_____

My mantra:

_____

_____

_____

Blend markings #1 and #2:

_____

_____

My Hand Analysis Blending Guide (cont.)

3. **Name of marking #3 I see in my hands:**

   _____

   Description of marking #3:

   _____

   _____

   Positive interpretation:

   _____

   _____

   Negative interpretation

   _____

   _____

   My mantra:

   _____

   _____

   _____

   Blend markings #1, #2, and #3:

   _____

   _____

Assignment 2
My Conscious Living Statement

THIS IS A SPACE to integrate what you have observed and written in your "Hand Analysis Blending Guide." You have three options for how to make this work for you:

1. Focus on using the mantras after acknowledging a challenge you identified, as in the example using the mantras in the previous "My Hand Analysis Blending Guide": *Even though I have been challenged with losing myself in the drama of others, [mantra] I am the love I seek and long to embody. And even though I am challenged with excessive analysis, [mantra] with an active mind, I am engaging life with clarity and consideration and communicating with compassion. Even though I have been challenged with my pattern of creating problems in relationships, [mantra] I claim my ability to engage in colossal complexity without creating tangled webs within my relationships.*

2. Clarify your challenges by identifying the negative interpretations in your "My Hand Analysis Blending." As an example: *My challenge with marking #1 is to nurture myself along with others without falling victim to emotional sell-out. My challenge with marking #2 is to be less critical of others. My challenge with marking #3 is to engage big enough and complicated enough problems to work on so that I don't create problems in my relationships.*

3. Focus on the positive interpretations you identified in your top three markings. Using the example assignment, you would say something like: *I help people feel loved and cared for, my mind is agile with the ability to examine, see, and comprehend from different perspective, and I have exceptional skill for synthesizing information.*

Do what supports you in the best way possible. This is for you to inspire you!

My Conscious Living Statement

Assignment 3
My Action Steps

IDENTIFY PERSONAL ACTION STEPS based on your discoveries here. Write down simple steps you'd like to take to improve in any area of your life, be it emotionally, mentally, physically or spiritually in relationships, career, family, or anything you think is important. You are encouraged to extend the strengths that you have become more aware of as you filled in the assignments to make them work for you. For example, you may have become more clear about how your natural emotional style (i.e., Heart Line type) can interact more effectively with someone special in your life and choose to communicate differently so that that person receives you better. Or you may want to take steps to enrich your spiritual practice or enliven your vocation. Don't worry about when you'll take action, just jot down the things you'd like to do as a result of your new awareness.

My Action Steps

Resources

Suggested Reading

Unger, Richard, *Lifeprints: Deciphering Your Life Purpose from Your Fingerprints*. Berkeley, CA, Crossing Press, 2007.

Mahabal, Vernon, *The Secret Code on Your Hands: An Illustrated Guide to Palmistry*. San Rafael, CA, Mandala Publishing, 2007.

Benham, William G., *The Laws of Scientific Hand Reading: A Practical Treatise on Scientific Hand Analysis*. New York, Hawthorn Books, Inc. 1946.

Sonack, Julie and Savage, Janet, *Hand Wisdom: A Holistic Guide to Hand Injuries and Your Health*. Colchester, VT, Little Cherub Press, 2013.

Visit www.AcademyofHandAnalysis.org to learn more about life purpose workshops, beginner's courses, certification programs, and associate faculty teachers.

Visit http://YourLifeIsInYourHandsBook.com

Readers

For the most current list of readers and consultants visit www.AcademyofHandAnalysis.org/category/Links

Newsletter

Subscribe at either www.KayPackard.com or www.AcademyofHandAnalysis.org

Jesse Hardy

About the Author

KAY PACKARD, M.A., is the founder and director of the American Academy of Hand Analysis. In 2003 she began formal training in non-predictive scientific hand analysis, after practicing astrology for the previous two decades. She has served as associate faculty at the International Institute of Hand Analysis. As a master hand analyst, she has read thousands of hands and taught hundreds of hours of hand analysis training courses to students from around the world. She received a master's degree in spiritual psychology from the University of Santa Monica in 2013. She offers life purpose readings using the science of hand analysis to individuals, families, and groups.

After traveling to India in May of 2010, where she was deeply inspired, Kay founded the American Academy of Hand Analysis. The vision of the Academy is to awaken and illuminate life purpose around the world and to expand awareness of the sacred and scientific advances in the field of hand analysis.

Kay is available to speak, host workshops, teach classes, and mentor individuals who wish to delve more deeply into who they are and what they are here to do. Please visit her website at www.KayPackard. com.

Kay and her staff appreciate hearing from you. Let us know how you have benefited from reading *Your Life Is In Your Hands*.

Notes

CPSIA information can be obtained
at www.ICGtesting.com
Printed in the USA
LVHW020436040523
745965LV00007B/305